MW01590876

Dedication

This book is dedicated to my father, Dr. Dan Moore Bechter. He passed away in March of 2008. Our visit to Newfoundland in the summer of 1996 was something special for many reasons. It was the last long vacation I ever took with him. His health began to deteriorate in his late 50s and early 60s, and he battled complication after complication over the few years he had after retiring from the Federal Reserve Bank. When his health started to decline I was working 80-90 hour work weeks as an equity analyst at Legg Mason after graduating from Darden. I did not have time to go on vacations in those first few years of my new career. I barely had weekends. I doubt he would have been able to travel anyway. As I mention in Chapter 1, our trip in 1996 inspired the return trip to the magical island of Newfoundland which is the subject of this book.

As an asthmatic, my father lived his entire life with the very real worry of something triggering an asthma attack. Going someplace far from the comforts of home, the nearness of medical care and the routines of his working life was no trivial matter for him. He loved to travel nonetheless. When I was young, our family took summer trips every few years. We went to the Grand Canyon and Carlsbad Caverns when I was in fourth grade when we lived in the Kansas City area. The second time I went to Canada – after the time my parents took me to Montreal for the World's Fair in 1967 – was over the summer just after my first year at the Naval Academy. My sister had just graduated from high school and was set to attend the University of Missouri and my brother had just gotten his driver's license after finishing his sophomore year of high school. We went to Ontario to camp, fish and explore. That was my first adventure in Canada. Lots of crazy things happened. We saw a dead black bear cub on an isolated piece of highway in the northern section of Ontario and stopped to check it out, all the time wondering if the mother was nearby. We caught northern pike hand over fist in a small pond next to the highway after fishing several times with no luck in the provincial park lakes. We took a train up to Moosonee on the James Bay through recently burned forest land, and my father almost got himself arrested at the border coming back into the United States because he was so eager to call my mother that he neglected to follow protocol.

I look back at all the vacations I have taken since then, most of them with my wife, and I realize that Ontario trip was the model I have followed ever since. My father taught me, whether I realized it at the time or not, to be more spontaneous, to let a trip take on a life of its own, to let it flow naturally.

So I dedicate this book to my father and I urge all fathers to take their kids places and to see and do things together. Do it while they are young and keep doing it as you get older. Get as far away from home as you can afford with the time and money available. See beautiful places and have the experiences together with those you love. I wish I had done much more with my father, and at the same time I am glad I did all that I did do with him.

Thank you, Dad, for giving me the appreciation for everything our entire beautiful planet has to offer and thank you for the time we had together.

Chapter 1 – A Little History

I had always loved everything Canadian since my youth living in Middlebury, Vermont, 100 miles from the border with Quebec, the French speaking part of Canada. My father taught mathematics and economics at Middlebury College while he was working on his doctoral dissertation in Economics. My parents took me to the 1967 World's Fair in Montreal when I was four. That was a major vacation back in those days of severely limited funds! I learned to love Canada's national game, hockey, as a young boy. My father took me to the Middlebury hockey games several times over the few years we lived there, and I was able to watch the Montreal Canadians, Boston Bruins and New York Rangers on television.

My wife, Libbie, and I had planned on getting up to Newfoundland over our honeymoon in 1990 when we took two weeks to see the Maritime Provinces, driving up from our new home state of Virginia. We had gotten married in Las Vegas in mid-April right after I got out of the navy and just a week after leaving my ship in Subic Bay in the Philippines. With my commitment to the navy completed, and my time as a naval officer over, Libbie and I drove across the country from Long Beach, California, where my ship was based, to resettle as civilians and start a new country life in Goochland County, Virginia. My parents and baby sister, who is nearly fifteen years younger than I, lived there. Before we were married, Libbie and I had bought a nice piece of land in Goochland that we would later build our house on. After giving ourselves five days of rest to recover from the cross country drive from California we headed north to my beloved Canada for our honeymoon of sightseeing and seafood. Neither Libbie nor I had ever been to the Maritime Provinces of Canada so we planned to see as much of them as possible over those two weeks.

We stopped to see the house my family had lived in along Long Island Sound in Connecticut. We stopped to see Bar Harbor, Maine and eat a fine lobster dinner. We saw the reversing falls in St. John and we camped in the Bay of Fundy National Park in New Brunswick on a night in which it snowed a couple inches. We drove around the entire province of Nova Scotia, using the city of Halifax and the town of Antigonish as centrally located home bases. We took the short ferry ride over to Prince Edward Island and drove around that entire province, making a point of checking out the beach on its north shore.

Unfortunately we simply ran out of time to make it up to Newfoundland, after checking out most everything worthy of being seen in New Brunswick, Nova Scotia and Prince Edward Island. Because getting to that island province required a long ferry ride we recognized about half way through our honeymoon that we were going to have to sacrifice some portion of our grand plan to see all four Maritime Provinces. Once we had made the decision to forego Newfoundland, I vowed to get up there as soon as life's events made it a possibility.

I made it to Newfoundland six years later. My father and I flew up to St. John's from Richmond via Toronto in the summer of 1996. We spent nine days in the province, with seven consecutive days in the middle of two weekends camping on the hard ground at different provincial park campgrounds. We spent the first and last day in St. John's, and I fell in love with the city – its people, its pubs and restaurants, and the incredible scenery from Signal Hill, truly a magical place. Away from St. John's I played golf at the incredibly beautiful Terra Nova golf course with my father riding along in the golf cart watching every shot I made and seeing everything I saw. We dined at Mom & Pop restaurants, holes in the wall and fishing village diners as we made our way around the island exploring. Our plan evolved daily. We made it west all the way across the island on the Trans-Canada Highway making it to Gross Morne National Park and its spectacular landlocked fiord. The trip provided my father and me some priceless time together and several special memories. It was without question one of the best extended weeks of my life. The trip also left me with a burning desire to go back.

Chapter 2 – The Challenge

Every year my wife's company, a chemical company headquartered in the Richmond area specializing in surfactants, phosphates and specialty industrial chemicals, put on an annual Christmas Party. The date for the party was always well ahead of Christmas, but still sometime in December. The 1998 party was held on a Saturday evening, the 12th of December. By 1998 I had been to five or six of these Christmas parties and had met most of the executives Libbie worked with as an executive administrative assistant. If Libbie saw somebody at these parties that I had not yet met she would make it a point to introduce me.

The Christmas party that year was held at The Dominion Club, a private golf club north of I-64 in the western suburbs of Richmond. It was an ideal location for a medium-sized company's Christmas Party. It had a large dining area in the main floor area over the pro shop and an expansive foyer that allowed for plenty of room for a company to set up a meet and greet zone for people arriving. Between the two areas Albright & Wilson had plenty of room for its over 200 local employees to bring spouses and friends to enjoy a holiday party celebrating the good year. 1998 had been a pretty good year for the company, and everyone seemed to be in exceptionally good spirits. I was feeling very comfortable at the party, having already chatted with several of the men and women I had come to know over the years and had just refilled my rum and coke at the bar when Libbie spotted someone that I had not yet met. She broke from a chat with one of her workmates when she caught a glimpse of Don Kretsinger, the company's logistics coordinator, standing not more than twenty feet from me. She gently tugged on my elbow to get my attention and motioned with her eyes for me to follow her across the room to meet Don.

Libbie made the introduction with one hand on my back and the other motioning between us. "Honey, this is Don Kretsinger; he is Albright & Wilson's shipping coordinator. Don, this is my husband, Timm." And with that she turned on a heel and went back to talking with a group of women.

After a cordial handshake with the customary "Nice to meet you" exchange, I curiously inquired "So what exactly does your job involve, Don?"

Don was about 5'8" with dark brown hair and a nicely trimmed and distinguishing short beard. He was very well dressed for the party, as most of the employees were, wearing a well-tailored lightly striped dark suit. I could tell he had answered my question many times over his career but he seemed genuinely happy to talk about his job. He replied as though he knew we would have more than a cursory discussion. "I make sure our products get to where they need to go and for bulk inputs I get involved on the supply side as well. I am a logistics guy, I guess you could say. We send most of our chemicals by rail but we also move some by truck and we get some of the raw materials for our plants by ship."

My navy background made me curious about Don's mention of shipping. I asked him what ports he dealt with for the ships.

"We have a couple plants up in Canada so we have ships transiting up and down the St. Lawrence in and out of Montreal and Quebec and in and out of Newfoundland," Don replied, exuding just a touch of pride in the company's broad reach geographically and his role in keeping everything going.

"Newfoundland? What port up there?" I responded quickly. Little did he realize how much I had fallen in love with the island province on Canada's eastern extremity.

"Corner Brook. We have phosphates that come down from Newfoundland into Virginia and those ships usually take something else back up," Don answered. I could tell he knew I was legitimately interested in the details because he was starting to offer up a little more than what I thought he normally would in a casual party conversation.

"I am a huge fan of Newfoundland," I explained, "I was up there for nine days with my father a couple years ago. We slept on the ground at seven different provincial parks over seven straight days in between nights at a B&B in St. John's."

"You know I have never even been there myself," Don replied in a somewhat dejected tone, almost lamenting. I think he realized how much I had enjoyed my experiences across Newfoundland's countryside and in its capital and largest city, St. John's.

"Don, you really ought to make a point of it," I replied, feeling it was sad he hadn't been up there. "The people are unbelievably friendly and the scenery is really something. St. John's is awesome. It's a beautiful place with a totally protected harbor and a big hill right at the entrance to it. And the bar scene is right out of fantasy land – live Irish music, big glasses of beer for a very reasonable price, incredibly friendly natives and visitors."

"I might one day, never know. I'm not much for travel actually...which is kind of odd I suppose given my job!" Don joked giving me an opportunity to change the direction of the conversation.

My brain had been knocked into a different compartment. Here was a guy who scheduled shipments by ship, train and truck and apparently hadn't ever ridden on any of the platforms he dealt with on a daily basis. I suddenly had an idea. "Don, I just had a crazy thought. Could you get a civilian on one of those ships you work with?"

Not surprisingly, that took Don off guard. "What do you mean? To look it over in port?" He asked me with a kind of puzzled look on his face.

"No. No. I mean to take a ride," I said slowly with emphasis on each word, hoping he would get how intensely serious I was.

"Where would you want to go?"

"Newfoundland." I said resolutely and without any reservation. He got my line of questions for what it was – a challenge from me to him.

"When?" Don asked, answering the challenge, signaling that he could make it happen.

"When is the next ship you know about going up there?"

"I'm pretty sure there is a ship leaving The Port of Richmond for Corner Brook at the end of the month."

I was surprised that it could be so soon, but it didn't take me long to realize that the timing might just be perfect. "Don, I am a graduate student up at UVA currently. We finish up the first semester in a week and don't come back for the second semester until January 11th." I paused to make a quick mental calculation. "I would guess it's five or six days to get up there – is that about right?"

I had been attending Virginia's Darden Graduate School of Business since the fall semester of 1997. My class, the Class of 1999, was close to putting the first semester of our second and final year into the books and I was thinking that maybe my best friend from Darden might want to join me if Don could pull this crazy idea off.

"No more than seven," Don replied. "I think they stop in Maine on the way up."

I wanted to make sure he knew I was not kidding around "Hey, Don, my buddy and I could absolutely do it. If you get us on that ship, I will deliver a case of beer to your doorstep."

Don took a long drink from his glass and hedged just a little. "I have never asked about it, but I don't know why they wouldn't say yes."

"Well Don – I am serious," I pressed, not letting up. "If you can get me on that ship, I promise you I will follow through. I can't promise you yet on my buddy, but I have a feeling he will want to do it." I had talked to my best friend at school, Mylan, several times about my trip with my father. I had used it as my story in a speech class in our first year. He had told me he would like to go there at some point. I doubted he had ever considered going up there in the middle of the winter, but I was pretty confident Mylan would join me.

Don was convinced I wasn't playing around. "Okay, Timm," he said. "I am taking this as a personal challenge. The only thing I ask is that you give me a full report when you get back."

He could have gotten a lot more out of me at that moment. I was excited by the thought of getting on a ship nearly nine years after getting out of the navy. "You got it. Don," I told him, "A case of beer and a full report." I took a few seconds to reflect on the prospects of being on a merchant vessel without a job to do. "While you check on it I will talk to my friend from school. When do you think you will know one way or the other?"

"I will talk to my shipping agent contact for that ship first thing Monday."

"Great. Just let my wife know when you get a definitive answer and she can e-mail me at school."

"Okay. I will do that." Don nodded.

I felt the urge to tell my wife what had just transpired. She would once again think I was nuts. She would probably hope Don wouldn't be able to make it happen. I was suddenly hungry. Excitement did that to me. I gave Don the most earnest parting best wishes for the season I had ever given anybody. "Don, I have never meant this more than I do now – it sure was great to meet you! Merry Christmas. I had better go find Libbie...and grab some food! Enjoy the rest of the party."

Chapter 3 – Let's Do It!

When I called Mylan and told him what had happened, he told me that if Don could get us on a ship, he was in. He hadn't planned anything special for the time after Christmas; he would just have to come back to Virginia a little early after spending Christmas with his parents in Baton Rouge, Louisiana. On Sunday I studied for my finals while watching NFL football games on television. With the first semester of the second year winding down, there were only a few classes remaining in the early part of the week before final exams. Mylan and I had a class on derivatives together on Monday morning, one of three we shared that semester. It was one of my favorite classes and one that we studied for together frequently. Our teacher was Bob Clark. He had already agreed to be our independent study professor and advisor for our second semester project. Both of us were doing well in the class and very much wanted to absorb all that Professor Clark was just about to put out in a final prep review session.

Professor Clark was just wrapping up the final lesson of the semester, a shorter lesson on combination strategies using multiple derivatives, before starting his 15-minute quick review prep for the final when the e-mail came into my inbox. It was from Libbie. "Don got you guys on the ship. You have to board early on the 30th, by 8am." She also added Don's phone number and suggested that I give him a call to make sure I got all the details.

I could barely contain myself but managed to remember where I was and refrain from shouting anything out loud. Mylan was intently listening to Professor Clark when I leaned over and motioned for him to have a look at my laptop screen and the e-mail message. He grinned at me and then nodded. I nodded back and gave a thumbs-up sign with my right hand where only Mylan could see it – right in between us just under the table that held our laptops. We both leaned back in our seats and started to let our minds wander to the unknown experience that lay before us. We had a hard time getting refocused as Professor Clark moved into the final review session.

After class ended I bounded out into the hallway. Mylan was right behind me. I turned to him. "Can you believe that? That Kretsinger dude wasn't shitting me – he did it; he got us on that ship!"

Mylan started laughing. "Now I have to figure out what clothes I am going to need up in Newfoundland in January!"

"That is a good point, MD." I said using his initials, one of my favorite nicknames for Mylan. "I think it is a safe bet that it will be pretty cold up there and you are going to want to have something warm to be able to be out on the ship too."

"I don't plan on being **out** on the ship much!" Mylan laughed more loudly. "You, Mr. Navy boy, can have all you want of that. I will be inside the ship reading a book until we get there!"

I knew he wasn't kidding. Mylan would very likely use the time on the ship as a time to read. His interest in the ship couldn't possibly be as strong as mine. I would want to see every inch of the ship and talk to all the crew about their jobs on it. "Mylan I am going to call Don and get a few questions answered. Do you have any questions?"

He paused a moment "Well, a couple I suppose. Try to see if you can get the schedule for when the ship gets up to Newfoundland so we can plan on getting back – that's a definite issue we have to work out. I don't know if you are thinking of flying back or driving or what, but we need to figure that out. Also we need to decide what we are going to do up there once we get there so we will probably need to rent a car. I will look into that – I can get a really good rate with Hertz. My other question is what are our sleeping arrangements going to be? Are we going to be in tight quarters or what? I may want to bring some extra bedding. I guess that's it. What other things are you going to ask Don?"

"I just want to get a better idea of the schedule the ship is on, more than when we get to Corner Brook." I said. "Also, I want to know how big the crew is, who the captain is, what will be expected of us as we hitch a ride, that kind of thing.

"This is just too cool." I couldn't help but say it. Then, just so that I knew without any doubt, I pressed him one last time. "We *are* doing this. Right, Mylan?"

He grinned big at me. "Yes, yes we are. Let's do it."

Chapter 4 – My Friend Mylan

In the second semester of the first year program at Darden all students were required to take a public speaking class known euphemistically as "Communications". Having been a plant manager I had spoken in front of my employees, citizens at public meetings and at events like Easter egg hunts and fund raising dinners. As a naval officer I had many times prepped my division of sailors, who, over my three years on board my ship, numbered anywhere from twelve to more than thirty. None of those speaking experiences prepared me for the stress of speaking in front of my classmates at Darden – classmates with high IQs and very judgmental attitudes, all of whom were indeed watching and judging, harshly. Watching my classmates present, I, too, was judgmental. So when Mylan got up and gave a speech about his experience as an attorney trying a case in front of a judge and held all of us spellbound, so impressed were all of us that we gave him a standing ovation after he finished. Many of us in the class, including me, were blown away by his demonstrated prowess for public speaking and actively lobbied the instructor to validate Mylan in the class and not let him speak again, lest he once again make all of us look grossly inferior by comparison.

It was after that day that I made it a point to get to know Mylan better. I really hoped that he would like to have a friend. While he wasn't quite my age he was closer to it than most of the other students – about three and a half years younger. He was from Louisiana so he was pretty far from home. I figured he might want to come over to my house over a weekend and watch playoff football so I invited him and another student, a younger guy who sat next to me in section, to come over for Sunday NFL playoff games. With my home about an hour away from Darden it wasn't like inviting them to some place close by. Luckily for me, both of them were eager to get away from their apartments for a change of scenery and different experience. We had a great time watching football that day and got to know each other a little better. The afternoon of football gave us a different environment to talk about things other than school – like what we wanted to do after graduation and what we had done prior to coming to Darden. As the second semester of the first year wore on and we got closer to summer, the first year program eased somewhat and Mylan and I, as well as others in our class, were able to get outside for a round of golf occasionally.

The game of golf, and the time it gave us to hang out together in that April and May of 1998, really cemented our friendship. It was on the golf course that I got to know how much Mylan loved the Fox cartoon show "The Simpsons." He used to quote Homer Simpson's lines from various episodes whenever something happened that brought one to mind. Over the summer between our first and second years, we communicated occasionally over e-mail keeping each other up on our summer internship experiences. Mylan had gotten an internship as an Investment Banker at Prudential in New York. I had gotten an internship as an Equity Analyst with Wheat First in Richmond. When Mylan finished up his internship in New York and moved back to his apartment in Charlottesville we wasted no time getting back out on Birdwood, the University of Virginia's challenging and beautiful golf course. With the more customized schedules of the second year program and the more flexible study hours that went with it, there was ample time to get out on the course one or two times during the week and almost always at least once over the weekend.

As Mylan and I became much better friends, we played other courses besides Birdwood in the fall of 1998 in our first semester of the second year. We began to study together for a few of the classes we shared, always at Mylan's apartment in Charlottesville. Mylan came over to my house a few times on weekends, and a couple times spent the night on a Friday or Saturday, depending on which day on the weekend we were playing golf and where we were playing. By the middle of the first semester of our second year, we had agreed to do one of our independent study projects together in the final semester. Mylan and I had grown to trust each other, to work together, and to enjoy each other's company.

Chapter 5 – Boarding in Richmond Harbor

My last final was on Friday the week before Christmas. I drove the hour long drive down I-64 home from Charlottesville immediately after. Mylan spent the night in Charlottesville that night and jumped on a plane to Baton Rouge the next morning. He spent nine days with his parents over the holiday period before flying back to Charlottesville late Monday. On Tuesday, Mylan drove over to our house so he could spend the night, leave his car in our parking lot, and join me when Libbie dropped us both off at the ship the next morning.

We woke around 5:30 am Wednesday morning and Libbie made us some eggs, sausage and toast. We had our large scuba bags fully packed and ready to go from the night before but had intentionally waited to load them into Libbie's maroon Bronco II until the morning. I had packed ten pairs of underwear, three pairs of jeans, several t-shirts to wear under sweatshirts, and three of my favorite sweatshirts, including a very heavy ski sweatshirt with a cinch-up turtleneck collar. That morning of December 30 was chilly but not at all brutally cold – a light jacket for 40 degree weather sufficed - but we had our heavier coats on for the weather further north later in our journey. We loaded up the Bronco at 6:30 am and were in the car fifteen minutes later driving down my long driveway through the woods and out to the main road.

The drive from our home out in Goochland County to The Port of Richmond took about 40 minutes. All three of us were tired from staying up too late and getting up early, not a good combination for early morning conversation. With Libbie driving, we mostly listened to the radio but did talk a little about how I would try to stay in touch with her over the course of the trip and what I had learned from talking to Don. The Ivan Gorthon would be carrying a full load of recycled newspaper up to Corner Brook. He had assured me over the phone that we would be treated well – the Richmond port agent he had talked to had promised him that much. When we got there around 7:30, Libbie jumped out of the car to see us both off. She gave me a big kiss and a long hug and then gave Mylan a nice friendly hug as well. We waved goodbye as she pulled away from the parking lot, leaving us very near the ship and the gangway that connected it to the parking area.

We turned toward the Ivan Gorthon and walked up the gangway ramp to board the ship. As Mylan and I stepped onto the deck, a man in his late 20's greeted us. "Welcome aboard, gentlemen," he said in an immediately identifiable Swedish accent. "I am Henrick Larsson, the ship's administrative and supply officer. The captain told me to expect you and show you to your stateroom. Captain Svensson would like to talk to you before we cast off, so please let me show you where you will be sleeping. I will let you drop off your bags and then I will take you to his office."

"Great!" we both answered at once.

Larsson, a toe-head blonde about 5'10" with chiseled facial features and a runner's physique, was dressed in a blue lightweight sweatshirt and jeans with a light tan zippered jacket. As soon as we had answered, he turned away from us and said, "Follow me." We hadn't walked more than a few paces before we got inside the first door, and he turned back and confirmed our names. "It's Mylan and Timm correct?"

"That's right. I take it Don Kretsinger got you our names somehow."

Larsson was quick and clearly prepared. "I deal with the port agent here in Richmond. Mr. Kretsinger deals with him as well. So yes, we did get your names from him I suppose, through the port agent." Larsson continued to talk as he walked toward the aft end of the ship through the central passageway. The passageway was amidships at the bottom of the superstructure that was well aft of centerline, nearly at the back end of the ship. "We are supposed to get underway about 8:30 am, and

Captain Svensson wanted to brief you before we do. He is going to advise you on where you can go on the ship and where you can't, when we eat and the safety instruction you will need to complete."

Neither Mylan nor I had given any thought to any training we might have to take. With all the training I had lived through in the navy I didn't give it too much thought but Mylan was intrigued. "What exactly does that involve – the safety instruction?" He asked me loud enough for Larsson to hear.

Before I could answer Mylan's question with an "I don't know", we had reached the stateroom where we were to sleep. It was bigger than I expected, bigger by 50% than the stateroom I had had on my ship, a frigate, in the navy. At the far end of the room against the wall, at the starboard or right side of the ship, there was a small desk with a chair with a porthole window looking out above. Bunk beds of ample width were to the right, just inside the door, and a sink with a mirror was in between the desk and the beds. Opposite the sink were tall narrow doors to a closet-like locker for hanging clothes.

Larsson first gave us his spiel on the stateroom. "You can hang your clothes in there," he said as he pointed to the closet, "and there are sheets and other bedding under the bottom bunk to make the beds. The hot water takes a while to come out, but be patient; it will eventually come out. You shower just across the hall – there are two showers in that room. The toilets are in there as well." He then turned to Mylan's question. "The safety training consists of some basic navigation instruction, cold weather survival suit training and abandon ship protocol instruction. It usually takes a couple of hours to complete and I would expect we will do the training once we get out to sea."

"Got it. Thanks for explaining that, Henrick," Mylan replied politely.

Larsson was not one for delays. "So, are you gentlemen ready to meet the captain?"

"I'm ready," I replied.

"Me too," Mylan added.

"Okay, follow me, gentlemen. The captain's office is up one deck and forward."

After a short walk up one ladder-like set of stairs and about 30 feet forward, Henrick Larsson knocked on the captain's door. "Captain Svensson. Our guests have arrived and are ready to speak with you."

The captain opened his office door and welcomed us. "Come on in, guys," he said with just a vague Swedish accent, "Have a seat." He motioned with his hand to the two chairs across from his desk in the modest 15-foot, nearly square, office. He then let Henrick go. "Thanks, Henrick; please let me know when we have all the paperwork ready."

Larsson replied in Swedish leaving me unsure exactly what he had said, but I figured the short quip must have just meant something like "Will do."

I was completely taken aback by how young Captain Svensson was. He was a good sized man at around 6'2", but he looked as if he could have just gotten out of college even with the slight paunch belly he carried. He wore glasses and had naturally wavy brown hair cut in a boyish longer style. He was wearing a white button down shirt with a sweater vest over it and khaki pants. His appearance reminded me of a rich kid dressed by his parents to come to the country club for Sunday brunch. I couldn't contain my surprise at his age and I am sure it showed on my face as I shook his hand on the way into the room. "Nice to meet you, Captain. My name is Timm."

Mylan, right behind me, the southern gentleman that he was, also greeted the young captain and shook his hand, but with an added token of respect. "Captain, nice to meet you *sir*."

I waited until both of us had sat down before I commented on the captain's age. "Captain, I have to say I am amazed at how young you are."

Svensson sat down at his desk. "Yes, I am a '98 graduate of the Swedish Merchant Marine Academy, and this is my first command. You are in good hands, gentlemen, don't worry. The Ivan Gorthon has a veteran crew even with its young captain!"

I was glad to know that he could so easily show a sense of humor. "So how long were you at the academy, if you don't mind me asking?" I pressed.

"It is two years with a year at sea between the first and second year. I am 25," the Captain answered politely.

"Well I am impressed," I responded. "In the U.S. Navy probably the soonest an officer could get command of a ship would be after seven or eight years of service, and that would be a small ship, like a mine-sweeper. I was on a frigate, a 440-foot escort ship with 17 officers and just under 200 enlisted crew. The captains I had were both late 30s, early 40s. I was about your age then. This ship is bigger in tonnage and you have fewer people to run it."

"True," he replied with a reflective smile and a little pause. "The difference, of course, is that this is not a warship. We need only get our cargo from point A to point B safely. And because we are running a commercial enterprise, we run with as few people as we can safely get away with."

"How many people, not counting us, will be on the ship, then, for this trip up to Newfoundland?" Mylan interjected,

"This is good," Captain Svensson said as he shifted towards Mylan, "this is one of the things I wanted to go over with you both. We have four officers and fourteen crew members. That is just enough to make this ship function while underway. We run four shifts of six hours each. We rotate half-way through the meal hour. We all eat together on a regular meal schedule – 6am-7am, noon-1pm, 6pm-7pm and midnight to 1pm. The crew does have its own mess. Cooked meals are not prepared for it, but food can be stored and consumed down there. If you want to eat off hours that is where you should go."

Sensing a purposeful pause, I took advantage. "Do you have us in officer's quarters? The room Mr. Larsson put us in seems pretty nice, and fairly large."

"Yes. We are fortunate that this vessel has more sleeping quarters than what is required by our crew. In the past, the Ivan Gorthon carried cargo that required additional crew so that is why we have extra berthing – enough space for you." He explained. He then picked up where he left off. "Okay, now for the rules for while you are on board. First the don'ts: Number one – at no time while underway is anyone allowed forward of the superstructure on the main deck. There is a safe outdoor area behind the bridge up high if you want to be outside while we navigate down river on our way out. Number two – while you will be allowed up on the bridge, I don't want you to interfere. I think this is common sense stuff and it will be pretty obvious what is okay and what isn't when you are up there. Number three – you can also go down into engineering if you like, and, as with the bridge, I simply ask that you don't interfere with the crew doing their jobs. Any questions on the don'ts?"

Both of us looked at each other wondering if the other had a question. Neither of us did. It *was* common sense, so we just shook our heads to indicate a no answer.

"Okay," our young Captain Svensson continued, "now for the dos: number one – We will conduct required safety training once we get out to sea. That will probably be late afternoon today. There will be an announcement when we are ready to do the training. The training is required, and you both need to attend. Number two – I want you to feel free to move about the ship and talk to the crew. All of the crew speaks some English, many speak English pretty well. You will soon meet everyone and see that our crew is Polish. They will want to talk

Timm Bechter

with you, I can promise you that. They are happy to have guests on board. It is not the usual, you see."

"How often do you make this trip, Captain?" I thought it couldn't have been too many times given that he had only been the captain of the ship for less than a year.

"This is my third time this year we have gone from Richmond to Corner Brook," Svensson answered. "This ship has probably done it far more than that. You can ask the crew how many times each of them has done it."

"I was told it is 7 days to get to Corner Brook Captain, is that correct?" I asked.

"That is correct, assuming the weather cooperates. Once we get around Nova Scotia, the seas can get pretty rough. We have to slow down in rough seas, so it may end up being a little more – we will see."

I could sense some worry in Captain Svensson's answer. It seemed a little odd that he would be worrying about weather when we hadn't even pulled away from the pier in Richmond.

"We will stop in Portland, Maine on the way and get a better read on the weather off the shore of Nova Scotia while we are in port," he continued, "Once we know the weather, we will have a pretty good idea of our arrival time in Corner Brook."

Mylan, who had been carefully listening to the back and forth, now was triangulating a plan for arrival in Corner Brook. "How long does the ship stop in Portland, Captain?" Mylan asked leaning forward.

"We will probably arrive mid-day and we get underway the next day late morning," Svensson replied without missing a beat.

"Will we be able to get off the ship in Portland, Captain?" I wondered out loud.

Our spectacled captain paused for a moment before answering, as if to consider how to keep the answer short. "We anchor when we first arrive and we move to a pier in the morning. I suppose you could get off the ship in the morning for a few hours, but I am not sure about that, actually. None of the crew will be getting off – that I am sure of."

I was satisfied that we knew what was ahead. Mylan was too. The captain was satisfied his guests had their instructions, their questions had been answered, and the rules had been laid out. He stood up; we stood up in response. "Timm, Mylan, please make yourselves comfortable on Ivan Gorthon. If you have any questions just ask any member of the crew. We get underway in about an hour. I will see you later."

And with that Mylan and I headed back to our stateroom to settle in, unpack, and discuss a few things.

"Too bad we can't get off the ship in Portland." Mylan noted as we got to the stateroom.

"Yeah. Portland probably has a few things we could check out if we could get off the ship. Oh well. Maybe we catch Portland somehow on the way back?" I joked knowing there was no way we would be hanging out in Portland on the way home.

"I doubt that." Mylan got my weak joke and gave a brief chuckle.

"Well MD, I am getting my camera ready for the ride down the James," I said as I opened the zipper into my yellow scuba bag. "And I am going to use the closet for a few of my clothes – might as well give them some air and get my bag out of the way."

Mylan took taking pictures pretty seriously and was way ahead of me. "Me too," he said, "I guess we can go up to that area behind the superstructure as we move down river. That probably will be the best spot to take pictures."

"We might want to take a few from the bridge too. Maybe we ought to head up there and scout things out a little before we get underway," I hinted. As a naval officer on The USS Vandegrift I had many times been Officer of the Deck when my ship had left the pier. My ship had bow thrusters, fancy jet-like thrusters that moved the ship sideways by shooting water out the side of the ship under water. I doubted that this merchant vessel would have such thrusters. I was curious how things would be done getting the Ivan Gorthon, a fairly large vessel, off the relatively short pier where the river was still fairly narrow. At this point, just a few miles south of the falls that ran through downtown Richmond, there was limited room to maneuver even as the James River was transitioning from a fast flowing, shallow river to something more like a narrow bay channel. The channel was dredged to adequate depth – I was confident of that – but that channel was not infinitely wide; it was pretty narrow. "I want to watch the process for getting off the pier and see how they work with the tugboat. I will probably take some pictures of that too, and I want to get an idea of how we can move around – you know, get to know the layout of the ship a little."

Mylan agreed that a few minutes scouting out the decks above us – the access to the topside deck, the bridge and whatever other vantage points there might be for taking pictures – was a good use of time before getting underway. We took about 20 minutes to carefully check out the ship. What we found was that the layout of the upper decks was quite logical. The center stairwell that had taken us to the captain's office continued up another level to access the bridge deck, which had the open, but safely railed in, outside deck behind it.

There was also a smaller observation deck over the bridge that allowed for an unobstructed 360 degree view. Up above the bridge there was no protection from the wind, and at this time of year that was a critical element of differentiation. An unobstructed 360 degree view was terrific, but if the wind was making it feel another 10 degrees colder, that could make the observation area behind the bridge far more attractive for the longer term periods of hanging out. I figured if we were going to use the top level viewing area, it would be for short periods, only in situations where it was paramount to be able to see all around.

After we had spent a good ten minutes or so getting our feel of the upper "weather decks," we moved back down to the levels of the ship that were indoors and out of the weather. We ran into a few of the crew and introduced ourselves quickly as we checked out the below decks, but at that point none of the names or faces really stuck with me. Under the deck where our stateroom was, essentially level with the main deck but inside the superstructure, we discovered the main dining area, the crews' berthing area, the separate crews' mess, and a long ladder down into engineering two decks below. We agreed to explore engineering later, once the ship was out at sea. Finally, and truly by accident, we found a door that opened into the main hold that gave us a mind blowing look at the ship's cargo – tons and tons of baled newspaper that almost filled the entire hold of the ship.

With our requisite tour of the vessel complete, we retired briefly to our stateroom to try out our bunks. We were still feeling the effects of having slept well under our normal number of hours and I was happy to close my eyes for a while even if I didn't go to sleep. Mylan insisted on taking the upper bunk despite my protestations. I had learned from playing golf with him and from studying with him that when Mylan had his mind made up, there was little I could do to change it, and this was one of those times where it was going to be his way.

Chapter 6 – A Slow Trod Down the James

The ship's horn blew, waking us from our brief naps. It took me ten seconds to calculate that I had been asleep for all of ten minutes. I got out of my bunk fairly quickly and looked back up into the upper bunk. Mylan had fallen asleep as well and was waking up a little less energetically than I had.

An announcement came over the ship's loudspeaker – "Underway." Still a little groggy, with such a short nap feeling like it had done more harm than good, the announcement sounded all too matter-of-fact to seem real.

Mylan moved rapidly to jump down out of his bunk after he realized that the ship was untied from the pier and was moving away from it.

"I don't want to miss this." I snatched my camera I had prepped ready to go on top of my half empty scuba bag on the floor.

"I am right behind you," Mylan said as he too grabbed his camera.

We climbed the stairs to the upper deck behind the bridge. We had decided during our scouting tour that we would observe the ship's movements chiefly from that vantage point while the ship was getting underway and over the multi-hour journey down the James River. It would allow us to see into the bridge through the charthouse to see how the captain and crew were interacting. And from there the view would be mostly unobstructed, except for directly forward, to see all around the ship. We crossed over to the side of the ship away from the pier and looked down.

We saw, just a little forward of the bridge, one lone tug boat rigged up tight to the ship pulling the Ivan Gorthon off the pier and moving her downriver. I couldn't help but notice how the river moved almost unperceptively in the deep water port just below the fall line in Richmond. Further up the river near where I lived you could walk across the river most of the time at depths from a foot to about waist high. You certainly felt the river moving when you were walking around in it or swimming in it where it passed south of Goochland County.

After a couple minutes the ship was far enough down the river that we could no longer see the port. The tug was untied leaving the Ivan Gorthon under its own power but the tug continued to follow alongside us. I was baffled. My curiosity was getting the better of me. I had to know what was going on with the tug. I decided it was time to go to the bridge. I figured Mylan would rather not go with me but I decided it was better to give him the choice as a courtesy if nothing else. "I am going to go into the bridge and find out what is going on." I said. "Wanna come?"

"No. You go ahead. I'm sure it's killing you not to be right in the middle of everything. You can fill me in when you come back." Mylan understood well enough what I was dealing with. I was feeling very out-of-the-loop not fully understanding what was happening. This was so completely different from having a job on a navy ship. I was either in engineering or on the bridge or in the combat information center when getting underway on The Vandegrift. Now I was a guest who had been told not to interfere. What a difference eight years and eight months had made!

I walked forward on the ship's large observation deck behind the bridge into the navigation room, often referred to as the chart room or charthouse. It had a large open area in the center of the room with several chart tables around its perimeter. It opened on both the port and starboard sides at its forward corners to the expansive bridge. With such a small crew and such a large ship everything about the Ivan Gorthon felt extra-large to me. Compared to my frigate the bridge was at least twice as wide and at least another half again as deep front to back. The charthouse was five to six times larger than the cramped charthouse/quartermasters shack we had on the Vandegrift. As I walked into the charthouse I saw a man making marks on one of the charts. Mylan and I had not run into this gentleman while quickly touring the ship a half hour earlier.

I figured him to be the ship's quartermaster/navigator. "Hello. My name is Timm. I am one of the guests on board for this trip up to Newfoundland. Am I interfering by talking to you?" I asked recalling Captain Svensson's request that we not interfere.

"No, no, you are not interfering at all," the man with curly hair and glasses responded in a slight Polish accent. "I just need to mark our progress as we move down river. These are all visuals, quite easy actually. I am Piotr. I am the quartermaster on Ivan Gorthon."

"Very nice to meet you Piotr," I replied extending my hand for a handshake, "If I can help you in any way please let me know. I am ex-Navy and I always enjoyed doing navigation."

"That is nice of you Timm, but I am okay. I can do the job myself," he replied overly politely.

"Very well. My instructions are to not interfere but the captain never said I couldn't help out!" I joked. "I am going to the bridge to see if I can get a better idea of what is going on."

"Well wait a second Timm, I can certainly explain what is going on." Piotr offered, surprising me.

"Okay. Well thanks." I returned. "So why is the tugboat not tied up but still moving along with us?"

"That is an easy one. That is the pilot's tug. Once he has gotten us down the narrow portion of the river then he will get off the ship and get on the tug and go back to the terminal in Richmond."

"Well, of course," I said, feeling kind of dumb for having asked the question. "I can't believe I didn't think of that. I never was Officer-of-the-Deck with a pilot on board when I was in the navy, although I think my ship used one a few times. How much longer will the pilot be on board?"

Piotr motioned for me to look at the chart he had been working with, "See here where the river opens up and we have navigation buoys the rest of the way?"

I was glad I'd had plenty of experience with charts. "Yes, I do."

"He will get off the ship right about here." Piotr pointed to the chart at a spot about a mile into the wider portion of the James about 3 miles past Hopewell, VA. "He will be debarking at approximately 9:45 am if things all go according to the normal plan."

"Very nice information, Piotr. Thank you," I said, sincere in my appreciation. Then, looking at the chart showing the James River all the way out to its exit in Hampton Roads, the area most in Virginia referred to as the Tidewater Area, I had a thought. "Hey Piotr, you have done this a few times right?"

"Yes, many times." He replied quickly realizing there was another question coming.

"So what is worth staying topside for do you think? My buddy Mylan and I have our cameras, as you can see." I looked down at my camera dangling from its strap around my neck, "What scenery is there on the way down the river?"

"You have come to the right place and the right guy. Here let me show you on the chart." Piotr again drew my attention down to the chart. "There are three really nice plantation homes on the way down you can get a very nice picture of all of them. Of course there are many other homes you can see on the river too. Right in here we usually see bald eagles." Piotr pointed to a stretch of the river near a wildlife preserve. "And then when we move past Hopewell you will be able to see all the chemical plants."

"Well I guess that is scenery of a different sort!" I laughed as I was fully aware of what Hopewell had in the way of belching exhaust stacks from the several chemical plants the city was known for.

"Once the river widens out, it does get less interesting really," Piotr warned, providing just the honest answer I was looking for. "You may not want to stay up here too long after we start moving without the pilot."

"How long to make our way all the way into the open ocean?" I wondered figuring that as helpful as Piotr was being he would have a pretty good answer.

"See this track?" He pointed to a very light pencil track that went all the way down the river. "That is the planned route. If we go our usual speed we should get to the first bridge coming into Hampton Roads about 1:20pm. From there it is usually about an hour to the Chesapeake Bay Bridge Tunnel. Now I don't consider that open ocean but it will start to feel more like open ocean once we get past there. Our next waypoint before we make the turn more towards the north is another 90 minutes further out to the east. We need to get into the shipping lane further off the coast." Piotr paused and stood up straight moving back away from the chart. "You know, you and your friend are lucky we are having such nice weather today. It could be below freezing and you wouldn't want to be up topside at all."

I knew he was right. The weather in Virginia at the end of the year could be fall-like, as it was today, or brutally frigid. You just couldn't predict it more than a week ahead. Mylan and I were indeed lucky. "You are right about that Piotr. Let's hope it stays this way."

"It won't." He said making it obvious to me that he knew what he was talking about. "By tomorrow it will be much colder and when we get into Portland it will be very cold indeed."

"Like how cold?" I asked remembering my younger years in Vermont when it could get well below zero Fahrenheit.

"Minus 30 Celsius, 10 below zero Fahrenheit. Very cold." Piotr did indeed have the forecast, as he would, being the ship's navigator.

I was chilled at the thought and glad Mylan and I had brought long underwear. It sounded as though we would need it and I figured that was a detail I had better tell him right away. "Piotr, thank you very much for all your help. I am going to head back and take some pictures and fill Mylan in on what you have told me." I said as I turned away from the bridge to rejoin Mylan on the aft deck high up in the superstructure of the Ivan Gorthon.

Mylan could see that I had stopped in the chart room and never made it to the bridge. "Who was that guy you were talking to?"

"His name is Piotr – P, I, O, T, R. Polish, which kind of surprised me. I figured the ship's navigator would be an officer and be Swedish. I was wrong about that. Very nice guy, and happy to clue me in."

"So what is the story with the tugboat?" Mylan prompted getting me back to why I had gone into the chartroom in the first place.

"We have a pilot aboard, which stands to reason. He will get the ship down the narrow portion of the river until a little past Hopewell and then he will get off the ship, get on the tugboat and then go back to the terminal in Richmond."

"Yeah, that makes sense." Mylan granted.

"He gave me plenty of other good info too. On the scenery he said there were three nice plantation homes to get good pictures of and he also said we might see some bald eagles along a stretch before we get to Hopewell. When we go past Hopewell he said we will get a good view of the chemical plants there – I hadn't even thought of that." Then I paused before giving Mylan the weather forecast. "This last tidbit isn't going to cheer you up, Louisiana man – it's supposed to get really cold starting tomorrow and when we get into Portland it is supposed to be ridiculously cold, like 10 below."

"Shit.   Well I guess we will be staying inside a lot." Mylan said remembering what the captain had said about the ship anchoring out once they got into Portland.

"One other thing, you just reminded me with that staying inside comment, Piotr said that there isn't much to see once we get into the wider section of river after Hopewell and before Tidewater. Probably want to just go back to the stateroom and do some reading or something once they let the pilot off the ship." I looked around while Mylan absorbed what I had said and realized that we had moved a pretty good ways down the river while I was talking to Piotr. "Hey, we are coming up on the Varina Bridge, the I-295 Bridge.   Do you remember it from when we played River's Bend? We should be able to see River's Bend golf course pretty soon." I said pointing up ahead to the right side of the river.

"I remember that bridge." Mylan responded. "When did we play River's Bend anyway? Was that this summer or was it since school started?"

"My memory says late September, after school started."   About two minutes later we could see a few of the holes on River's Bend – the green on #1, the entirety of #2, and the tee box on #3. And then the modern, center line supported, Varina suspension bridge was dead ahead and the ship was moving at a fairly good clip down the straightaway section of the river closing quickly on it. The bridge would be the first of several landmarks we would see over the next few hours. We climbed the ladder up to the observation deck over the bridge on the ship to go under the bridge over the river. I was transported back to the time in 1988 when the Vandegrift had been asked to participate in a ship parade, a regatta, up in Astoria, Oregon. I had been on the ship's bridge for our approach into the harbor and we had gone under a beautiful bridge coming into port.

This was different in two ways – I had driven over the Varina Bridge in a car many times. I had never driven over the Astoria Bridge. The other incredibly obvious difference was that this was a merchant ship moving down a relatively narrow river, not a warship moving into a seaside harbor. In both cases going under a bridge on a ship is an instant lesson in perspective. The underside of a bridge is something you rarely get to look at and the Varina Bridge, built just a few years before, was a beautiful piece of engineering, both from the top and the bottom.

After passing under the bridge our scenery turned to nice homes along the river, not plantation homes but nicer more modern homes, some with elaborate stairways down from the bluff to the river where the owners had docks and boats on the river.

After a while longer a large power plant was visible up to the right, and later a sand and gravel operation with a barge loading facility at the river's edge.

Suddenly there was a bald eagle overhead looking down at the ship. As we were looking at it and getting ready to take some pictures Piotr came out of the charthouse briefly to point out the wildlife preserve up ahead. "You will likely see many more gentlemen," he predicted confidently.

Mylan made a point of greeting Piotr then with a quick introduction and handshake. He didn't want to spend too much time on formalities or small talk with the chance of good photo opportunities of bald eagles pending. Piotr seemed to want to get back to the navigation room anyway, so the interaction was short.

Over the next 15 minutes Mylan and I counted nine different bald eagles soaring overhead and nearer the bluffs to the south side of the river. They were harder to see over nearer the refuge to the north, where they flew lower to the trees, often landing in them. Only once did we see an eagle dive on the river for a fish, and it came up empty that one time. For the eagles it seemed rather more of a day for flying than for catching a fish.

"That was worth the ride right there – seeing all those bald eagles," Mylan reflected as the Ivan Gorthon neared Hopewell, "They are so effortless in flight. It seemed like they just wanted to fly around. Most of them stayed up high and over by the bluffs."

"Agreed, my friend." I sighed. "And to think they are only a few miles from Hopewell – enough to make you appreciate how far we have come in this country to have wildlife and businesses coexist." I couldn't help thinking about how DDT had nearly made our national bird, an iconic symbol of our country, extinct and how we humans figured out what the problem was and fixed it. And now, not more than five miles from Virginia's chemical manufacturing center, there were many bald eagles flying around.

Just then the first of the large plantation homes came into view on the port side of the ship. It appeared just upstream from where an old bow in the river rejoined a cut through. Smaller boats were able to use the cut through but not larger ones. This first plantation home was Shirley Plantation – a three-story cube-shaped multi-window mansion with just a small opening cut through the trees along the river to see the estate.

"See that?" I pointed towards the house on Shirley Plantation so Mylan could locate it right away. "Pretty sure that is Shirley Plantation...pretty *surely* it's *Shirley* Plantation."

Mylan shook his head at my pathetic play on words. I had had too long to think about it since looking at the chart with Piotr and simply could not resist the humor reminiscent of one of my favorite comedy movies *Airplane*. "Boy, *surely* hope the humor gets better from here!" Mylan quipped as he drew his camera to his eye for the first of several shots of the plantation.

And so it went down the first seven to eight miles of our trek down the James River, Mylan and I pointing out various sites of interest to each other – homes up high on the bluffs, nice ones and not so nice. Another plantation home and a few other large homes of more modern vintage came and faded behind them as the Ivan Gorthon moved down river with its Richmond-based pilot steering the ship through the several windy turns the river took getting to Hopewell – the city of chemical plants.

As we made the final turn in the river, before it opened up past Hopewell, the city's many chemical plants began to come into view. Hot gases rose from the stacks at the four or five largest plants – steam from a few, sulfur laden yellow gases from a couple, greyish gases from yet another couple.

Sharing with Mylan some perspective from my seven years working with state environmental regulators and various environmental attorneys over my career with the lightweight aggregate company, I commented to him. "This town gets a lot of attention from the regulators – EPA and state environmental both. When you see what comes out of these stacks, you wonder what it was like before we had environmental laws."

"There are towns like Hopewell in Louisiana and Mississippi too. We need the chemicals; life wouldn't be what it is for all of us without them." Mylan stated matter-of-factly. It made me realize that Mylan's career as a corporate attorney had given him an appreciation of both sides of the issue. I had learned a long time ago what a measured and informed attitude Mylan had toward just about every issue. This was no different.

"You are right, brother," I agreed. "Reminds me of that movie where the guy is running around saying 'Plastics' to everyone – what movie was that anyway? Was that *The Graduate*?"

"Yeah, I think that's right," Mylan responded, barely giving me or the question a thought.

We agreed that once the ship got past Hopewell and let the pilot off the ship we would retire below for a longer nap and some reading before the ship made its way into the Tidewater area. The 10 minute naps we had snatched before the ship had gotten underway had done little to satisfy our sleep deficit.

It was nearly 10 am when we got back to our stateroom. The fresh air topside was only increasing the frequency of the yawns that had started when we had awakened that morning at 5:30am back at my house. We had made a point of having a full breakfast but that now seemed like quite a while ago. We were already thinking about food and realized when we came in the door of our room that we would be hungry before noon – the advertised time for lunch. I set my little travel alarm for 11:45 and we agreed to grab some food before getting back up to the bridge deck for the transit through Hampton Roads. I looked forward to seeing all the bridges and bridge-tunnels that would split up the transit's last hour before we left the river and nearby land behind. Once we left the mouth of the Chesapeake Bay through the Chesapeake Bay Bridge Tunnel we wouldn't see land again until we came into Portland, Maine on Saturday, three days later.

Chapter 7 – Into Open Ocean

The alarm I had set went off right at 11:45 and for the third time that morning we woke up. For me it was a personal record. This time I felt fully refreshed and ready to experience the last stretch of the transit down the James River through Newport News, Hampton and Norfolk. Mylan immediately reminded me that lunch was number one on our agenda. Our growling stomachs could no longer be ignored; it was time to see what kind of lunch the ship had to offer on our first day on Ivan Gorthon.

When we got to the dining room nobody was there. We looked around the room. Sure enough, the countertop just opposite the kitchen had a sandwich making spread out on it – lunchmeats of all varieties including some hard sausages, four types of cheeses and three types of bread. There were a few small bowls of condiments as well – mayonnaise, mustard, pickles, relish and fresh lettuce.

"Down right American, this spread." I noted, expecting something Swedish or Polish I suppose.

"Yeah, it is, kind of," Mylan concurred but then added, "But sandwiches are fairly universal." He then built himself a modest sandwich. I, on the other hand, went full out Dagwood and built a double stacked, three slices of bread, monster of a sandwich with every lunchmeat and cheese on the spread. We sat alone at the table big enough for 16 people and ate deliberately. I figured since the ship was moving down river lunch was going to be a little off of whatever was normal, then again we were a little early. Mylan and I didn't really talk much at all as we sat there. We simply tried to eat as quickly as possible. As big as my sandwich was and as slow as I eat that was a challenge. We figured we had about an hour-and-a-half before we left visible land behind.

Not long after noon, this time with full stomachs, we were back on the observation deck behind the ship's bridge and charthouse. The first road bridge the ship came to coming into Tidewater was the James River Bridge. It had a massive gearing system to lift the center span from both sides to allow the ship to pass while the cars waited. Again I was struck by how totally different a perspective it was to see a bridge from underneath. Seeing that gearing system from the underside got me thinking about how such massive metal parts were made, transported and installed. We humans could accomplish some pretty amazing things when we worked together and used heavy equipment.

The next "bridge" didn't qualify as a bridge from the ship's perspective because the bridge portions of the bridge/tunnel were on either side of the tunnel we passed over. This was the I-664 bridge tunnel, the major interstate route loop on the western side of the Tidewater area. I had driven over the bridge portion and in the tunnel portion at least ten times since moving to Virginia. It was a strange feeling to know that the ship was moving over cars underneath us in the tunnel. The next bridge/tunnel was much like the first from the ship's perspective. The I-64 bridge tunnel, the eastern portion of the loop around the Tidewater area, also had a tunnel in the middle for ships to pass over. Again the Ivan Gorthon passed over the tunnel without fanfare – no cars had to stop at all – they just drove under the ship, through a tunnel, made by well-trained engineers and construction personnel, under the water. The harbor was getting bigger and bigger after the I-64 bridge/tunnel; the land on either side was getting further and further away. Up ahead was the final bridge/tunnel, the granddaddy of them all – the Chesapeake Bay Bridge/Tunnel – 13 miles of bridge and two long tunnels, one for inbound ships to go over and one for outbound ships to go over. As we passed over the tunnel with the entrance and exit to it on either side of the ship I couldn't help but express my joy at being on a ship again. "Mylan, my friend, out to sea we go. I love it!" Mylan just shook his head and laughed.

With the ship past the Chesapeake Bay Bridge/Tunnel the Ivan Gorthon had another 90 minutes east bound before changing and heading to the north. We looked backwards as the Chesapeake Bay Bridge/Tunnel faded in the distance behind the ship's wake. The Ivan Gorthon was now at full cruising speed.

"Let's go talk to Piotr and see the course he has plotted to get to Portland," I said to Mylan once the Bay Bridge Tunnel was nearly out of view.

"Maybe he will know when we are doing the safety training," Mylan added.

Piotr was on the bridge with the Captain, and they were discussing when to hold the safety training when we made it through the charthouse and onto the bridge. Mylan and I waited patiently near the starboard side door into the bridge as Piotr and Captain Svensson discussed the afternoon schedule. We could hear the conversation well enough that we caught the end of the back and forth when Captain Svensson decided that 4pm would be ideal. That took care of that question we had planned on asking. Piotr had what he needed from the captain and the captain had what he needed from Piotr. Piotr turned back toward the navigator's chartroom through the door we were standing in. We stepped aside and followed him back into the charthouse.

"Piotr," I said as he settled in over the chart that had the course plotted all the way to Corner Brook, Newfoundland, "would you mind going over the course up to Portland with us?"

"No problem." He replied, motioning for both of us to lean in over the chart. "We will make 20 knots so figure about 480 nautical miles per day. By this time tomorrow we should be about here, about 100 miles off of Nantucket Island. Our waypoint here is where we turn from 035 degrees to 000 degrees, due north. We will slow to 10 knots at that turn so we arrive in Portland harbor at the prescribed time of 4pm on the 1st.   We turn from 000 to 285 here for our last 8 hours into the mouth of the Portland Harbor."

"Thanks Piotr," Mylan said. "I guess we will see you at 4."

"You will," Piotr responded. "See you guys then."

With about three hours until the safety training we headed back to our stateroom to read for a while. The day to that point had been pretty full for Mylan and me, even though we hadn't been required to do anything except meet with the captain. The journey down the James and out into the open ocean through the busy population center of the Tidewater area had been, at various points, educational, entertaining and scenic. I was ready for a little quiet time with a book before our first required evolution – the safety training.

Chapter 8 – Safety Training

It turned out, not surprisingly, that Mylan and I were the only two people on the ship who had not had the training before, but several of the ship's crew made a point of coming up for the training nevertheless. The captain had put Piotr in charge of the training and it consisted of three major parts, all of which were designed to prepare those on board for the event no one ever wanted to happen – an abandon ship situation. Part one was location awareness. Part two was life boat knowledge. Part three was the survival suit.

Because we had already reviewed the track the ship was going to take with Piotr, he chose to make cursory work of that portion of the training and began instead with a lecture on the importance of knowing the nearest point of land.

"Should we have to abandon ship the captain, I, or the officer of the deck, will make every effort to inform the crew and our passengers of the nearest point of land," Piotr started in a way that made it clear he had done the training more than a few times. "We mark our location every ten minutes, at a minimum, so if you have an opportunity to look at the large scale chart at any point during our transit you may already have a pretty good idea of how close, or how far away, the nearest point of land is. During daylight hours we will also note the position of the sun relative to nearest point of land. At this time of year the sun is at a near extreme position south, arcing from approximately 55 degrees south of east to 55 degrees south of west. Sun up and sun down is posted in the charthouse over there and the lifeboats do have laminated smaller scale charts in them with floats attached. Any questions so far?"

Mylan and I were mum – so far so good. It was all sinking in. To me this was all common sense, although I was both curious and amused at how the training was different from how the navy trained for such an unwelcome event. In the navy, with the chain of command, and the far greater number of people on board the ship, certain individuals were given greater responsibility for lifeboats, their contents, and the procedures necessary, should their use become mandatory. It was commonly accepted thinking that the only way navy personnel abandoned their ship was if it was sinking under them; otherwise it was the ship's crew's duty to save the ship. And navy personnel spent hours training on how to do damage control. I knew from personal experience, having run the daily training for over two months prior to a Persian Gulf deployment on the USS Vandegrift.

On my ship we spent far more time practicing saving the ship than practicing abandoning the ship. So I had to keep things in context and in perspective. Of course everybody on board a navy ship was expected to know how to release a lifeboat, but the ones on my frigate were not as large as the ones on Ivan Gorthon, and there certainly weren't as many people on the Ivan Gorthon as there were on my frigate. The other factor that could not be ignored was that the Ivan Gorthon was heading up to the North Sea in the winter. So despite all my mental notes on how this training was so different from what I had experienced in the navy, I was laser focused. It was all new to Mylan. As he was in class at Darden, he was all ears and fully engaged.

Piotr continued, "Okay, so now let me review the lifeboat launching sequence. Let me say, Timm and Mylan, that God forbid we would actually need to abandon ship, I would fully expect a seasoned crew member to be taking care of launching the lifeboats, not either of you. In any case, to launch the large lifeboats one can use the electric motor system, assuming we have power, or the hand crank, if we don't. Let's go outside on the bridge wing so I can show you where these controls are." With the wave of his hand Piotr had us follow him out on the bridge wing.

The rest of the men who were with us for the training stayed inside. While we were out there, he pointed out both the control panel on the bridge wing and the local control panel right next to the 25 foot long Boston Whaler-style hard bottom boat. The Boston Whaler would be, by far, the best option should the crew be required to abandon ship. It had a motor and room for the entire crew. There were two such lifeboats, one on either side of the ship. The controls for the lifeboat winching system were about as simple as one could imagine – raise and lower buttons with lights indicating positions as fully raised, boarding level and fully extended. It was clear that the lifeboat could, and now and then did, function as a captain's boat to get people to shore when there was no other means available. It made me more comfortable to know that the Boston Whalers actually got used now and then. The ship also had four canister-packed inflatable rafts as "emergency lifeboats" – they were set on pressure release triggers to detach from the ship and inflate automatically should the ship actually sink and the water level of the ocean come up to meet their positions on the side of the ship. Piotr made sure that Mylan and I were aware of them as well, before the three of us walked back into the charthouse.

When we returned to the group, Piotr took on an even more serious tone. "Okay, Gentlemen, now for the fun part of the training – survival suits. These suits will save your life so I want you to take this very seriously. At this time of year in these waters up here in the North Sea...well we aren't up there yet, but even here off the U.S. coast and off the coast of New England and the Canadian Maritime Provinces if you fall in without one of these suits on you will be dead within a few minutes, forget about the ship having time to come about and pick you up. So don't fall overboard! Okay, so both of you have suits assigned to you. Surgei will help you, Mylan, and Czeslaw will assist you, Timm. I want you to put these suits on two times – once with help and once without any help."

The survival suit, bulky and florescent bright orange, came in a box like package with a Velcro sealed flap. Surgei and Czeslaw showed Mylan and me how to pull the flap open with deliberate force and then pull the folded suit out of its soft case. Surgei worked with Mylan and

Czeslaw worked with me to show us how to unfold the suit and climb into it feet first. It was immediately obvious how this heavy suit worked to keep a man alive in the frigid water. The suit material was like insulation and rubber combined, soft and spongy but firm and solid like leather, all at the same time. It had air gaps between the inner lining and the outer orange rubber-like skin that allowed for the wearer to blow air into the suit to both keep himself afloat and insulated from the cold water that would otherwise sap all the heat out of the body. It took a few minutes just to get into the suit on the first attempt. The final and most important steps of pulling the hood over the head and the gloves over the hands were details that Sergei and Czeslaw made sure both Mylan and I understood clearly. They looked us straight in the eye to make sure we were paying complete attention and absorbing the techniques. This was clearly serious business, and it was obvious to both of us that our crew helpers thought it was a life or death matter. Maybe the seriousness of the matter made for nervous laughter, who knew exactly, but as serious as both of us realized the training was, we could not help but laugh once each saw what the other looked like in these amazing orange suits. We were one step away from looking like a nutty mascot at a minor league baseball game with our faces just barely peeking out of the hood and our hands covered with mitts. We took pictures of each other and smiled for the camera, keeping the mood lighthearted, but everybody present realized that the survival suits were no laughing matter in the event they were needed.

Sergie and Czeslaw helped Mylan and me out of the suits and showed us how to fold them up and return them to their large pouches. On the second run we were on our own. The cameras were put away. We were all business. Sergie, Czeslaw, Piotr and the other three members of the crew there to observe the fun and get a refresher stood around us in a rough circle saying nothing. Piotr, I think, would have yelled at any of them had they kibitzed at all. Once Mylan and I had gotten ourselves completely into the suits again, including donning the hood and tying it up tight to have only our eyes and nose showing, and pulling the mitts onto our hands, Piotr was satisfied that we knew what we were doing. In the interest of time, and probably in some measure out of politeness for us as guests, Piotr asked Sergei and Czeslaw to once again help us out of the suits. Once we had them off they also helped us fold them and put them away again. Piotr joked that the next time we had to put the suits on getting out of them would be the reward for living. I made a quiet promise to myself that there wouldn't be a next time.

Chapter 9 – Meals with the Crew

Over the remainder of our first day on the ship, December 30th, and the next day, the final day of 1998, December 31st, Mylan and I interacted heavily with the crew. Starting with dinner, not long after our safety training, we ate four meals over four shift changes with the ship in full underway mode. With no more than ten people eating at a time the dinner table, which sat sixteen, it was never completely full. The meals were interesting times of human interaction for Mylan and me as observers. There were conversations – some in Swedish, some in Polish, a few in English. When the officers wanted to talk to the crew, or visa-versa, they used English. When the crew members were talking to each other they usually used Polish but now and then would insert English just because the word or phrase was better for the situation. It made us aware that even had we not been on board, the crew would have used English now and then – sometimes out of necessity and sometimes just because English provided a better way of saying something than the speaker's native language, Swedish or Polish. It was a lively and interesting environment indeed.

The first dinner included fresh vegetables and steak, kind of a kick-off-the-cruise treat I figured. Mylan and I got a chance to talk with a few crew members from engineering who had stayed below watching over the engineering plant during the outbound James River portion of the trip. The men encouraged us to come down to the engineering area of the ship to have a look around right after dinner. Mylan agreed knowing I would certainly join him.

After downing the fine meal, recounting the fun of putting on the survival suits with the guys at the table, and hearing a few stories from the guys about sailors who had survived because of their survival suits, Mylan and I followed Johan Marski, a young slender engineer, down the several ladders from the dining room to the engineering room. The engineering room consisted of a large grey wall of panels full of knobs and gauges monitoring all the various systems associated with the electrical and propulsion systems of the ship. Everything was powered by multiple diesel engines. In that room were a couple of well-padded chairs for the crew members standing watch. The control room was walled off from the diesel engines, but by no means was it completely quiet; the diesels could still be heard. On the panel wall in the center portion, where there were a couple sections without gauges or knobs, there was a large calendar with a naked woman and a laminated poster of all the ships in the Gorthon line – nine different hull types in the company's fleet of 18 ships. We spent over an hour asking questions and learning about how the various diesel engines powered the ship's propulsion plant and its electrical distribution system. In addition to Johan we also talked with Boris Linka, an older seaman who said as little as he could get away with, more out of personality than because of language issues. He made light of the work involved with keeping the Ivan Gorthon's engines going, giving the impression that he had been doing the job for so long it was not in the least bit difficult for him.

After the educational time we spent with Johan and Boris low in the aft end belly of the ship I felt the urge to get up to the bridge to see the stars before calling it a day. The weather was still fairly nice for late December. It was close to 9pm. However, with Piotr's weather intel in mind, and a slight cool breeze out of the northwest starting to become apparent, it wasn't hard to imagine that this would be the last evening of mild winter weather to enjoy the clear sky out at sea. With a cursory look at the chart to see that the ship was now well off the coast of Delaware, more than 50 miles out to sea, Mylan and I went through the door from the charthouse onto the bridge.

George Preudhomme, the most ethnically interesting man on the ship, was at the helm. George's father was from Grenada, a small Caribbean island, and his mother was Polish. He spoke Polish, English, and French fluently, and enough Swedish to converse with the Swedish officers fairly well. George's father was a merchant sailor and had spent a good deal of time in Poland prior to meeting George's mother. George's complexion was somewhere between a fair skinned Jamaican/Caribbean and a well-tanned Italian. His hair was salt-and-pepper. He wore auto-dimming glasses and was stubbornly partial to summer clothing, no matter the weather. Out in the ocean with the sole task being to keep the ship on a particular heading, conversation was welcome by most all helmsmen, and George was happy to tell his story. In exchange for telling us his background George was curious to know how we had managed to get ourselves on a merchant ship for a trip to Newfoundland and why we would want to do it in the winter.

I explained how Libbie worked with Don Kretsinger and how Don had worked with the Richmond port agent to get Gorthon Lines to okay our journey north on Ivan Gorthon. George remarked that Captain Svensson was quite early in his career and was more than a little apprehensive about the whole idea of having civilians on his ship. When George shared this about Captain Svensson, I felt compelled to tell George about my navy background. I believed that it must have made it easier for Captain Svensson to agree to let us come aboard. George agreed that my background was probably a big positive. After talking with George, we took a good look around the bridge and spent a few minutes studying the ship's radar imagery, learning how to control the range of the radar scope. We then went back to the open area behind the charthouse for a little fresh air and a look at the stars. Until you can see the stars from the ocean out of the light pollution of land you haven't seen all the stars you can see from planet Earth. Mylan and I took several minutes to identify as many constellations as we could before heading below to our stateroom for our first night of sleep under the sheets of our bunk beds.

Sleep came easily with our stomachs full, our minds tired from a long day of sensory stimulation, and the satisfaction of feeling welcome on the ship. By 10:30 our stateroom was dark and the battle of snoring buddies was naught – both of us were too tired to let the other's sinus obstructions hamper a good night's rest.

We didn't bother setting an alarm for the morning of the last day of 1998. We both woke up around 6am. With a warm shower and a hot breakfast of sausage, eggs, toast and sausage gravy we got the day off to a great start. One thing caught our attention that morning as we enjoyed our breakfast; as part of the breakfast spread, Mylan and I both noted the availability of cold cuts and sausages on the counter exactly where they had been the previous day for lunch. The sausages were different from the breakfast sausage. These were like kielbasas, larger in diameter than a link breakfast sausage, and partially sliced up. There were three different kinds along with the various cold cuts. We made a mental note to keep checking the counter at every meal from that point on.

I elected to spend more time in engineering that morning and Mylan elected to read.

Lunch was cold cuts and cheese sandwiches with ample chips of a few different varieties and the same sausages that were present at breakfast. Having noticed that the same sausage was out for breakfast and lunch today and for lunch the previous day we decided to monitor its consumption over the entire lunch period. Since neither of us was expected to stand any formal watch the monitoring was easy for us to do. We stayed in the dining room that day until the cook cleaned up. It did not take but this one lunch period to realize that this sausage was an essential ingredient for the Polish crew members. Each of them took some of the sausage over the lunch period. If this magical sausage had caffeine in it or had religious significance of some sort it would have made more sense to us. I pledged to get to the bottom of the story before the end of the trip – to understand the importance of this special sausage.

Over the afternoon I joined Mylan in the stateroom to read and to pen a couple post cards – one to Libbie and one to my mother. Before dinner

I spent some time on the bridge and in the charthouse. The temperature outside had turned colder as Piotr had said it would. Sergie had the helm and for the thirty to forty minutes I was up there talking with him we did not see a single other ship.

During the final dinner of 1998 several members of the crew invited us to join them in the crew break room for New Year's Eve partying. And, yes, again the sausages were part of the dinner spread.

Chapter 10 – New Year's Eve, 1998

New Year's Eve 1998 and where were we? Mylan and I were on the Ivan Gorthon, a 380-foot long Swedish merchant vessel with its hold full of bulk newspaper. The ship was riding low in the water moving through fairly calm seas and cold crisp air about 100 miles off the coast of Massachusetts. We were just over halfway to Portland, Maine, our one and only stop after leaving Richmond, Virginia, en route to Corner Brook, Newfoundland on the western coast of the easternmost province of Canada. Mylan and I were temporarily oblivious to the conditions outside, our position in the ocean and the ship's cargo. We were completely focused on the celebration transpiring in the crew's mess on the last evening of 1998.

"My turn." I tapped Mylan on his left shoulder. It was evident to me that he needed a little break from the arm wrestling contests being wildly contested in the crew's mess low in the Gorthon's belly. Mylan had already been in at least three different contests. He ceded his seat to me at the white Formica-topped table usually used for quick meals and snacking off normal meal hours. I sat down to take on the lanky and wiry strong Johan Marski who had barely won out over Mylan after a protracted back-and-forth battle. Mylan moved over to where I had been sitting to the left and grabbed his glass, still curiously full of vodka. Oh yes, vodka, straight, the virtually taste-free spirit known the world-wide and an obvious favorite of our hosts. He drained it.

"Son of a bitch!" Mylan shouted out quite uncharacteristically after draining his glass, "I just got tired out, Johan; rematch tomorrow!" Mylan had won his first two matches but had succumbed most likely out of fatigue to the fresher Marski, the strapping young engineer of probably 22 or 23. Mylan, ten years, maybe more, Marski's senior, long and lean and wiry strong himself, was a fierce competitor, he didn't like to lose no matter the sport. From the Gulf coast, born in Mississippi and raised there and in Louisiana, his education and professional demeanor belied his southern roots to some degree. But here in this raucous environment he briefly let out a little of his inner fire. From behind him Boris Linka quietly refilled Mylan's glass.

Mylan had clearly worn down the young Johan Marski with their extended battle and I, on my first match, made quick work of him. As an old baseball player, if there was any part of me that was overdeveloped, it was my forearms. I also outweighed Mylan by forty pounds, despite giving away an inch or two in height. More than once I had been jokingly referred to as Popeye by our classmates at Darden. Of the forty pounds extra I carried compared to Mylan maybe a pound was in my forearms. The rest was distributed in my thicker frame, the genetics I was born with for which I blame my mother and the rest in my belly, genetics and bad habits for which I mainly blame my father.

In the confines of the crews' mess, with the various conversations ongoing amongst the men, there was always another sailor waiting to test his strength against the reigning arm wrestler of the moment. I had waited for Mylan to lose before jumping in. Taking Johan's place was the older and bigger deck hand Surgei Rocamalev who was closer in age and in size to me. I was within a month of my 36th birthday. I figured Surgei was probably closer to Mylan's age than to mine. Since we had gone through safety training, we had gotten to know many of the men a little better. Surgei was one of the more interesting sailors on the ship. He didn't look much like a Russian despite his name. He claimed that his paternal grandfather was Ukrainian-born but had moved to Poland after WWII and that all three of his other grandparents were Polish. "Okay Surgei, settle on in, I'm just getting warmed up here," I challenged while grinning a large devilish smirk. "What the hell time is it anyway, guys? Gotta be getting close to midnight!" I knew we were getting close to midnight even though I was not wearing a watch and there was no clock in the room.

Mylan, still on my left, had started up a conversation with our navigator, Piotr. Piotr, close to Mylan in age and of all the Polish crew, likely the closest in intellect, was on a roll taking about his native land. Behind his circular framed glasses and under his curly hair was one impressive cerebral cortex. As Sergei and I got our match started I could hear Piotr turning the conversation to Polish politics – whether Poland should be admitted to NATO and to the European Union. As I looked over, waiting on Sergei to get comfortable, I could see that Mylan was totally engaged and was starting to drink with little awareness of pace and quantity.

As Mylan and Piotr's conversation intensified, Surgei and I were straining in a left-handed arm wrestling match that seemed more like an isometric exercise – there was no movement away from the vertical starting position, just shaking and quivering. We both grabbed the table with our right hands and braced for leverage as our faces turned red with strain. One of the crew, I couldn't tell who, shouted out for Surgei to put an end to it. "Finish him off Surg!" he shouted.

About a minute into the match, I started to make a move and had moved Sergie off of vertical by a couple inches. I felt if I could pull down and get an inch or two every time I sensed an opportunity I could finish Sergei. Just then Czeslaw, the man who had helped me don the orange survival suit, clearly full of excitement for the clock to strike the magic hour, made an announcement in English in his heavy Polish accent, "Five more minutes to midnight!" That was all it took to destroy Surgei's concentration and give me the victory.

"Anybody else?" I inquired of the remainder of the crew, sensing that my match with Sergie might be the final match of 1998.

Piotr did not hesitate to take the lead of his fellow crew members. He suggested convincingly that rather than continue with the testosterone drenched arm wrestling, everybody fill his glass with vodka in preparation for midnight. "No more wrestling. You can do more after midnight, you guys. Fill up now and we make toasts!"

Mylan and I complied and checked to see where the levels were in our glasses. Mylan's needed another dash or two. Mine was already full. Having been engaged in the last arm wrestling match Boris Linka was seeing to that.

"Okay, I start," Piotr said once he was satisfied everybody was ready with a full glass and paying attention. "I wish to make a toast to Poland and its membership in NATO – that it will happen in 1999!" Everyone raised his glass toward the middle of the table as we all gathered around it standing. "Skoal!!!" Piotr shouted and everybody repeated, with Mylan and me lagging only slightly.

Czeslaw was next and it was clear that he had been eagerly waiting for the moment when he could make his toast. "To America! Poland's friend, land of milk and honey, home of the brave, home of the free!"

I was flabbergasted with Czeslaw's toast, full of several of America's catchiest proud phrases and couldn't help commenting before the glasses were raised. "You have been doing some reading my friend, very impressive!" and with my added comment glasses were again raised to the middle of the table. "Skoal!!!" the men shouted out even more emphatically than before. This time Mylan and I were not late to the cheer.

Mylan, the orator extraordinaire I knew him to be, looked around the room. I could tell he was feeling the effects of several glasses of vodka already consumed but his talents could not be restrained. He had been motivated by the political discussion with Piotr, his toast made that clear to me. "To Poland, to America, to a healthy Europe with Poland as an important part – and never again any wars in Europe." Mylan could always inspire me so I felt compelled to add a sincere "Hear, hear." I almost said "Amen." And then Czeslaw screamed "Skoal!!!" like a high school kid at a pep rally.

We were really putting away the vodka.

There were a few more toasts – not as bold or as political – mainly about women the sailors knew or were married to. It was fun to see the crew having such a good time and to be part of it. Mylan and I were having a great time. And, as thankful guests invited to join the festivities, we drank along.

With the toasts over and the clock now solidly in 1999, Mylan joined Piotr in a game of checkers. I went back to arm wrestling for a while, starting with a right handed match with Sergei. I don't remember the other matches that night.

Somewhere around 12:30am Mylan excused himself abruptly from his game of checkers with Piotr. "Gentlemen I am done; calling it a night." I heard him say as he slowly got up from his seat. I watched him leave the mess and thought about saying I was right behind him, but I didn't.

About an hour later I retired from the party as well and stumbled back to our stateroom oblivious to the path I took. In my first effort to be conscientious in 1999, as pointless as it likely was to my unconscious buddy in the upper bunk, I did not turn on the lights as I came into the stateroom. I stripped to my underwear and climbed into my bed, the lower bunk. As far as I could discern from below Mylan appeared to be sleeping soundly above in the upper rack. Horizontal at last, I was out cold in five seconds.

Chapter 11 – January 1, 1999

Mylan woke me around 8 am. "Timm, hey, wake up." He spoke forcefully down at me from the upper bunk just loud enough to wake me but not too loudly. I was on my back, no doubt snoring. I could feel it in my throat. I didn't like to sleep on my back and rarely did. It was the alcohol. I don't suppose I turned over all night after going lights out in seconds after lying down at nearly 2am.

I opened my eyes and weakly got out a "What?" barely able to form the word.

"I got blood all over the place up here," Mylan informed me in a strangely matter of fact tone. "I sliced my finger somehow and bled all over the wall and the sheets and pillow. Funny thing is that my finger isn't bleeding anymore." Mylan paused, I think waiting for me to say something.

I was listening but just barely. What I was thinking was that I didn't feel very good. After a couple seconds he calmly asked me, "Hey are you awake?" wondering if I had gone back to sleep.

"Yeah, I'm awake," I responded, starting to understand that I was indeed awake, but that I was better off sleeping, and that he had just said some things about bleeding all over the place. I told him "MD, I feel like crap. I think I am going to puke as soon as I get up."

"Well don't rush it if you can help it." He suggested sympathetically. "I am going to need to get something to clean up this wall. I am getting down. Stay put a second."

Mylan, sporting a white tee shirt in addition to his boxers, turned his body from a sitting position and gracefully lowered himself feet first to the edge of the lower bunk and then to the floor.

As soon as Mylan's legs appeared coming down from his bunk above mine my bladder screamed at me as if had been rudely awakened by a nightmare. "Man, I have to pee something fierce, Mylan. Let me get to the head," I said, climbing out of my bunk in nothing but my boxer briefs. Mylan barely had time to get his feet on the floor but managed to move to the center of the room and sit down in the stateroom chair quickly enough that I didn't knock him down.

I made a beeline for the head across the hall. I almost didn't make it. I felt as though I might explode, there was so much pressure. As soon as I was in front of the toilet I quickly began emptying my bladder. Within a few moments I was also emptying my stomach. Thank God no one was there to witness my lurching and heaving. I would have been a sight to see, bent over puking while trying to pee. Luckily no one was there to see it. That was my personal test to know if peeing and puking simultaneously was possible. For me it wasn't. My firm view, to this day, is that it is physically impossible to pee while puking, but eventually, after a few stops and starts, I had accomplished both and returned to the stateroom. While nowhere near normal I felt much better. I was lucky being a German-Irish American that I could drink and not get the crushing headaches many people got as part of a hangover. For me it was just a stomach issue. I turned my attention to my roommate.

"So what did you do to cut your finger?" I asked Mylan as I opened the door to the stateroom.

"Hell if I know," he responded. "I can't believe it bled that much. I guess vodka thins the blood."

"Yeah, it probably does." I laughed looking down at the pile of my clothes crumpled on the floor just where I had left them before crawling into bed. Mylan let out a little laugh of his own. I knew he wasn't laughing at the same thing but I didn't know then what had him chuckling. "Man, I don't even remember getting back to the room last night, Mylan. We drank way too much."

"No shit, navy boy," Mylan said somewhat in exasperation. "And I am not feeling like doing much today. I need some time to recuperate I think. Do you think you could round up some stuff for me to clean up the blood on the wall?"

"What do you want me to get exactly? Don't you think soap and water would get that out?" I asked looking at the streaks on the wall above Mylan's upper bunk.

"Yeah I do. Probably just need a few clean rags and some mild soap. I can use the water from the sink here in the room," Mylan replied making a face that had *hangover* written on his forehead.

"Alright MD – I will round that stuff up and get back here as soon as I do," I said pulling on my jeans.

I put on the rest of my clothes and went to the dining room to see if I could get the rags and soap from the cook, Mikolaj Bartowski, known to everyone on the ship as Miko. He was just finishing up his clean up from breakfast. Thanks to his responsibilities for feeding officers and crew both, Miko was one of the few people in the ship's crew who did not stand an alternating watch schedule. He also had, without a doubt, the least command of the English language of any of the Polish crew.

I was feeling just stable enough to deal with Miko after the hard night of drinking and my comic scene in the bathroom puking my guts out. I greeted him quietly as he was putting dishes away. "Miko, hey. I need some soap and water." I motioned with my hands like I was washing my hands. I looked at him to see if he understood me. I felt he had to know the word water. He looked at me as if I was speaking Greek. Had he been a dog his head would have been cocked over.

I tried a slightly different approach. "I need to clean up, Miko. I need to scrub with soap and water." This time I motioned with my hand that I was cleaning the counter. I paused again to gauge his reaction. I wasn't sure if he understood so I made a motion of squirting some liquid soap onto an invisible rag and again motioned like I was scrubbing the counter. "Scrub... with soap and water... with a rag, a cloth... clean." I looked back at him again and sensed that he had it this time. He turned and went over to the storage closet in the kitchen. I was relieved to see him come out with several wash rags.

He handed them to me and said in slow chopped English, "You clean with these."

"Thank you Miko." I replied nearly bowing in gratitude. "Soap? Liquid soap? Dishwashing soap?" I asked looking at him while making a motion as if I was squeezing liquid soap out of a bottle into the rags now in my right hand.

"Okay. Yes," Miko replied. He took a few steps to the side and reached into a cabinet under the main big sink in the kitchen. Sure enough he pulled out some dishwashing liquid soap and handed it to me.

"Good! Yes. Thank you Miko. This is what I need. I will bring it back to you later. Thank you." I had never had to make such ample use of the words "clean, scrub, soap and water" just to obtain cleaning materials. I could have earned a Boy Scout badge for impromptu sign language before it was all said and done. In the end it was mission accomplished. I emerged with several clean rags and some liquid soap. I had successfully communicated with Miko about something unrelated to food, no minor accomplishment.

When I got back to the stateroom Mylan was back in bed.

"Hey, you all right?" I asked looking up at Mylan back in bed.

"No." Mylan answered, clearly not in much of a mood to talk. "I puked again. I feel like if I stand up I will probably start to dry heave. Just better for me to lie down I think."

"You puked *again*?" I asked making it clear a little detail would be appreciated.

"Yeah. Again." He confirmed and then added the detail I wanted to hear. "I got out of bed in the middle of the night. You were out cold. I just vaguely remember that. I barely made it across the hall. That I remember quite well. I was probably in there for ten to fifteen minutes heaving my guts out into the shower. The whole experience I would just as soon forget, but it was so unpleasant I don't think I ever will. That God-damned vodka had its revenge. Hell, it's still having it. I do think this is the drunkest I have ever been. I was probably every bit as drunk at 4:30am as I was when I went to bed. I'm still polluted. I can feel it still. It's a damn good thing I purged my stomach so my blood alcohol level could have a chance to start moving in the downward direction."

There was bright sunlight in the stateroom now from the window at the far end. With the ship on a due north course, 000 degrees, the rising sun was coming in from its southeastern angle on our starboard side stateroom. The sunlight was both good to see and somewhat unwelcome as the bright light was both a reminder that a new day had dawned but also painful for eyes and heads feeling the effects of a hangover. I knew it was cold outside but at that moment all I could think was how glad I was we had comfortable bunks, a warm stateroom, and a cover for the window. I stepped over to the porthole window and pulled the cover over it to block the sunlight.

I really didn't know what to say about Mylan's mid-morning stomach purge. I felt for him. I knew how I felt, and I had a feeling he had consumed more than I had. I could hold my liquor normally and I had puked myself. "Want me to clean the wall?" I asked not sure if that even made sense since he was now back in his bunk. I just felt I had to offer.

As I expected he declined. "I will do it. My blood after all. Maybe in a little bit I will feel up to it."

"Okay, I will leave this stuff in the sink then." I said putting the washcloth sized rags in the sink and placing the bottle of liquid soap on top. I then looked around the room and considered what to do next. I didn't feel like hanging out with Mylan as he dealt with what I figured was borderline alcohol poisoning. I always figured the best way to get back to normal after a hard night of drinking was to act normal until you felt normal again. I decided to go outside and check the chart in the charthouse to see where we were. "I am going to go get some air." I let Mylan know. "I want to see where we are and try to get my appetite. I'll be back after a bit. Just try to sleep some more – that's probably the fastest way to get back to feeling normal."

After wishing Mylan some more rest, I exited the stateroom and made my way up to the charthouse behind the bridge to check the large scale chart. The 8:45am mark had just been plotted and it showed that the ship would be coming to a 285 heading and aiming at Portland harbor at approximately 10:30am. From my navy experience I knew that there had to be a smaller scale chart with the plot for the last legs into Portland harbor. I had been watching Piotr at every opportunity and had a pretty good idea where he might keep such a chart. I was right – it was under the lift table in the storage space just under the table top and it was right on top. With a quick glance I made note of the planned arrival time – 3:30pm, five hours from the change of heading and well after lunch and before dinner. There would be a break from underway until morning and that meant the ship's crew would get a break from the normal watch schedule. I also realized that the ship would average a slower speed over the last 60 nautical miles as it came in closer to land. I wanted to be on the bridge for the approach into Portland. I wondered if Mylan would be feeling better by then or not.

Armed with the course and timing of the ship's approach I moved forward to the bridge. Captain Svensson was sitting in the Captain's chair. It was the first time I had seen him there.

"Good morning, Captain," I said, forcing an energetic greeting despite feeling less than full of energy.

"Good morning, Timm," Svensson replied somewhat flatly. "Where's Mylan? I heard you guys did some serious drinking with the crew last night over the midnight hour."

"This is true." I answered, drawing it out some. "Some arm wrestling, some chess playing, some checkers, many toasts, more political discussion than I ever dreamed – really had a good time. Stayed up pretty late. I think I went to bed close to 2am. Not feeling the greatest to be sure. Mylan is still in bed actually. He is not doing so well. I think he drank quite a bit more than he realized, victimized by the behind the back, fill your glass pouring of the stealth Boris I am afraid."

"He is known for that, from what I hear, Boris Linka I mean..." Captain Svensson mused. "Tell Mylan I hope he feels better soon."

"I will. So we anchor today, Captain?" I replied wanting to change the subject.

"Yes. There is another ship at our pier. My understanding is that they will pull out early in the morning. We will moor after they are out of the way – probably no later than 8am. We will be underway once they are clear of our path to the pier," Svensson answered anticipating my additional questions.

"That gives your crew some down time then. That's kind of nice to have I would think," I offered.

"It is. We can all get a good night's sleep tonight. I think plenty of the crew need one after last night." Captain Svensson laughed.

"Good point, Captain. Somebody must have been thinking when they made the schedule for Portland..." I laughed along with him politely.

I decided I didn't really feel well enough to keep talking with the captain and headed back out through the charthouse and back to the open observation area behind it. The temperature was now well below freezing outside and the fresh air had both an invigorating and an unsettling effect all at once. I was instantly fully awake and suddenly just as nauseous as I had been when I had climbed out of bed an hour before. I moved quickly back to the rear of the observation area holding back the first gag fighting its way up my throat. Within a few more steps I succumbed, vomiting once again.

As luck would have it - or the fact that the first round had pretty much emptied my stomach - there was little to puke out this time. I was glad for that. With so little expelled I had little concern of cleaning it up. The final contents of my stomach froze solid on the deck in just a few seconds. I hoped no one had seen me gag and spit. I snuck a look back at the charthouse to see if Piotr or anyone else was there watching me. No one was. I had had enough of the cold air and, amazingly, now felt that maybe I might be able to find something to eat that would agree with me – yogurt or toast or something. With that thought in mind I headed back down to the dining room so see what Miko had left out after breakfast. I hadn't even thought to look when I had gone down to get the soap and rags a few minutes earlier.

On the counter in the dining room were two loaves of bread, the now fully expected Polish sausage, some cereal, milk, and some yogurt in plastic containers. I stared at each item on the counter in sequence several times hoping one would say something inviting to my stomach. The meditation eventually led me to drop a couple pieces of bread into the toaster. I thought I could probably keep some toast down along with some yogurt. Yogurt had settled my stomach before in my life – after late nights out drinking and in the mornings a couple times after major binges when I was at the Naval Academy. The one I always remembered was when I woke up in a hotel room full of people after the 1984 Army-Navy football game in Philadelphia. Like last night I hadn't been able to piece together how I had gotten in that room either.

I put two pieces of the whiter bread in the toaster and opened up a blueberry yogurt. I pulled up a chair at the table to sit in while I waited on the toaster. I slowly spooned the yogurt into my mouth all the while considering how yogurt might just be the perfect post-drinking morning food. In a couple minutes the toast was ready. I was feeling better fast and within about five minutes I had consumed my light late breakfast. It was just enough to get me back on track to feeling normal after the night of vodka.

When I got back to the stateroom I peeked in and found that Mylan was indeed asleep. That was definitely for the best, I figured. I didn't feel like reading or hanging out in the room while Mylan was asleep so I decided to head down to engineering to see who was down there and how they were doing.

I opened the hatch to engineering and walked into the control room. Neither of the two men on watch, Boris Linka and Johan Marski, both of whom had stayed up later than I drinking and talking, even bothered to turn toward the door. They were barely functioning after the hard night of partying. I could tell immediately that conversation was not in the cards so I decided to head back up to the bridge. The captain had left the bridge and only one man, George Prudehomme, manned the helm.

"Well, good morning, George. How are you doing today?" I inquired quite sincerely, wondering if George had gotten involved in any partying himself.

"I am fine, Timm. Just another day for me. No drinking for me last night. I have to drive you know." George responded totally understanding the reason for the question.

Wondering if Mylan and I were at the only booze fest on the ship over the New Year's turn I asked "So was the party that Mylan and I attended down in the crew's break room the only one on the ship last night? Do you know?"

George did know. "The officers gathered in the captain's office last night and had a toast and some food but it was not a party by any means. I was invited, which was nice, but I was only with Captain

Svensson and Larsson, Svard and Johansson for about 15 minutes. With only five people you can't really have much of a party."

"Yeah, that's a good point. Nice that the captain did something to recognize the New Year though," I commented, thinking it would have really sucked to not even acknowledge the New Year just because you were an officer. I reflected quickly on the manning of the ship with its four Swedish officers and fourteen Polish crew and wondered if what kept them separate last night was their pay grade or their nationality. Then I realized the young captain had been nice enough to invite George to the short but sweet gathering of the four officers for some reason. Why I wasn't sure. I decided to leave this question alone for the time being. I wondered if being underway over New Year's was common. I remembered George had been a merchant marine sailor for many years. "How many New Year's Eves have you been underway for, George? How do they usually get treated on a ship?"

"Pretty much how you experienced it I suppose. From what I hear you guys had a pretty good time last night. Piotr was telling me that Mylan was pretty wobbly and that you didn't call it a night until close to 2am." He paused as I nodded in confirmation and then continued. "I have been involved with that kind of deal several times, probably four or five. I would guess I have been underway for at least ten New Year's Eves. The older I have gotten the more likely I have skipped the partying. Kind of got sick of feeling sick I guess." George leaned back in the helmsman chair as if replaying all of the times he had imbibed over New Year's on cruises gone by.

I looked out at the ocean ahead of the ship and thought about all the times I had drank as much or more as I had last night. I could count the number on both hands. "You know, George I can understand you deciding to take the watch and pass on the partying. I haven't been much for partying on New Year's Eve myself over the last many years. Last night was amazing in how easy it was to drink. That Boris kept the glasses full and everybody was in such a good mood. The vodka just went down way too easy."

George nodded as if to say "Been there, done that."

"Any of the crew feeling really bad this morning?" I asked figuring if anyone could tell me it would be George. Of course I had already run into Boris and Johan who had been partying with Mylan and me and the rest of the crew and I knew they were barely functional.

"A couple of the men were feeling it but they got up and got going." George replied not using any names.

"Hey George, how come you weren't up here when I was up here about an hour ago?" I suddenly thought to ask, remembering my visit to the bridge earlier in the morning when I had spoken with the captain.

"I had to help Larsson for a while – putting a few things together for Portland. Surgei spelled me for that time. He was up here wasn't he?" George double-checked.

"Yes, he was." I answered only vaguely remembering. "I only talked with the captain and I wasn't up here that long – really was just getting my sea legs under me at that point."

George and I continued our conversation for a while longer, discussing what Portland and Corner Brook had to offer a tourist in the winter. I then retreated back to the stateroom. When I got there, Mylan was awake but still in bed. He was on his back with the sheet over him.

"How are you feeling, MD?" I asked him.

"Not good. I think I may have gotten close to alcohol poisoning last night. I haven't felt this bad since I...well, never. How in the heck did I let myself drink so much?" Mylan asked rhetorically to the ceiling just above him as he lay prone in the upper bunk.

I noticed that he had cleaned the blood off the wall and elected to mention that fact while answering his rhetorical question. "I think you can blame it on Boris. He was filling your glass and everybody else's after most every sip or slug. People tend to drink more if they don't realize how much they are drinking. And vodka, well it doesn't get much easier to drink than vodka – after a while almost like drinking water – unfortunately it ain't water. I see you managed to do the wall."

Mylan wasn't in much of a mood for talking but managed to explain to me how the wall washing probably set him back, "Yep, didn't really take too long. I wish I had waited now though because that exertion just made my head hurt worse and standing up even for just those five to ten minutes was enough to put me back into dry heaves."

"Well shit, Mylan," I cursed out of exasperation. "I could have done it." I felt as I would have, had my wife tried to lift a heavy weight and thrown out her back.

"I know," Mylan responded. "It's done now."

I grabbed the book I had brought along for the cruise, "*The Gorilla Game*," and sat at the desk at the end of the stateroom under the porthole window. "You mind if I turn on some music?" I asked Mylan.

"I would rather you not," he said. That was further confirmation that he really was not doing well at all. Mylan usually wanted the music playing, and it was he who had brought the medium-sized boom box on board.

So while Mylan lay in bed I read in silence as the ship heaved ever so slightly in the long but steady deep water waves off of Maine.

At 11:30 I went down to lunch and ate a light meal. Mylan did not get out of bed. I saw Captain Svensson again and again he asked about Mylan. I told him that Mylan was not doing so well and that he was still in bed trying to get over one of the worst hangovers he had ever had.

After lunch I went back to the stateroom to continue reading. After reading a couple chapters I even managed to take a short nap. By 2pm I was feeling close to normal. The ship was just off the coast of Maine and within a few minutes of maneuvering into Portland Harbor. After reading another chapter of my book I headed topside. This time, knowing I would be on the observation deck to take pictures in the bitter cold, I put my ski jacket over my ultra-heavy ski sweatshirt I had purchased on a ski trip in Vermont a couple years before. With camera in hand I was ready to snap a few pictures as the Ivan Gorthon came into Portland Harbor.

It was darn cold when I got out on the observation deck. I had to keep my hands in my pockets when I wasn't taking a photo. But it wasn't the cold that was putting a damper on my enjoyment. It just wasn't the same being on the observation deck behind the bridge and charthouse without my classmate and friend, Mylan. Without him to share the experience Portland Harbor seemed all the colder and all the darker. I hoped Mylan would get back to normal soon.

The approach into Portland Harbor was uncomplicated. There were no other ships moving around, and the Gorthon needed only to drop anchor somewhere in the middle of the harbor to spend the night. The weather was calm but extremely cold. Water vapor rose from the harbor in an eerie steam-like way as if from a hot tub. If over land, it would have been fog and someone would have been making a vampire movie. The water was probably only slightly above freezing but it was far warmer than the air, itself closer to zero in Fahrenheit terms. Once the Ivan Gorthon had anchored I went back below to the stateroom to take off my coat and sweatshirt and sit with Mylan, hoping he would be up out of bed and up for dinner. It turned out he wasn't yet ready to eat but he was out of bed – a major improvement for sure – and he was reading the book he had brought along for the cruise, "*Buffet,*" the Warren Buffet biography.

"Hey, hey! You are out of bed." I exclaimed as I came in the door playing my favorite superhero, Captain Obvious. "Think you could keep some dinner down?" I asked him optimistically. I was hoping against my expectations my roommate would say yes.

"I don't think so. You go ahead to dinner without me. Maybe I will feel up to eating a little later tonight – I am feeling better; the pounding in my head and the dry heaves are gone; at least I can get out of bed." Mylan grimaced as he answered.

I was disappointed but not surprised. I had hoped that lunch would be the last meal Mylan would miss and I would not have to explain his absence once again. I had a feeling if I saw Svensson at dinner he would ask me about Mylan again so I decided to tell Mylan about lunch. "The captain asked about you again at lunch. If I see him at dinner what do you want me to say about how you are doing?" I asked feeling I needed a little input from Mylan just in case.

Mylan looked up at me and cocked his head in frustrated bewilderment. "Hasn't he ever had a hangover before?" Then, as quickly as he had let himself vent he calmed himself, as if realizing that he probably should give me something. In his lawyer tone he told me, "Just tell him I overdid the vodka – that is the truth – and tell him I will be back to normal in a few more hours – pretty sure I will be."

"All right...I am big on the truth. He seems to be pretty interested in your health today. That is what I will tell him." I plopped back into my bunk with my book.

At 5:30 I headed to dinner. I had a real appetite again. I was starving. I was completely back to normal. I was ready to eat in serious fashion. Mylan stayed in the stateroom. He had been alternating between sitting at the desk reading and lying in his bunk reading. I was feeling encouraged when I left the room because Mylan had the stereo boom box playing. I took that as another sure sign of improvement. I felt confident that he would be eating something before the day was done.

Captain Svensson was already at the table when I arrived. All three of the ship's other officers – Henrick Larsson, Gustav Svard, and Olaf Johansson – were seated at the table and George and Piotr too. Clearly being at anchor was a different situation than being underway when it came to presence at dinner. "How is Mylan? Is he coming to dinner?" Captain Svensson asked before I could sit down.

I remained standing to answer as everyone at the table listened. "No Captain, he is not. He told me to tell you that he is pretty sure he will be up and about before the day is done. Just overdid the vodka last night. He is reading now in our stateroom. He is out of bed."

"I am concerned about him," Captain Svensson said flatly. He then turned to Miko who had just come out of the kitchen. "Miko – let's have the salad."

With the captain's request for the salad to be served, the meal had begun. I took a seat next to George and across from Piotr about mid-table with the officers on my right. With the ship anchored the captain had put Miko into a more formal service model, bringing the food to the table rather than having it put out on the counter for a buffet.

All but one seat at the table was taken as the meal began, and by the time the salads had been consumed, it too had been filled. Had Mylan made it, I wondered what that final crew member would have done. Would he have waited to eat until someone was finished? Would he be squeezed in somehow? It was academic. I let the thought go. Most of the crew of the Ivan Gorthon was eating in the early shift, most likely to allow for an early night into bed.

The main course of chicken fried steak, potatoes and mixed vegetables followed the salad. It was great to have the food at the table instead of on the counter. It was too bad Mylan was missing this meal – probably the best one the crew would enjoy on the way up to Newfoundland. The officer side of the table initially started a discussion of the weather – not the weather in the port but rather the weather around Nova Scotia. Piotr was involved in the discussion so I had a good seat to take it all in. The seas were heavy according to reports coming in from Piotr's navigation resources.

Most of the conversation was in English as the officers discussed the weather with Piotr. I wondered if this was for my benefit. Conversations broke into smaller groups as the men settled in to enjoy their meals. Again mostly Polish on my left, mostly Swedish on my right. I talked with Piotr and George across and next to me and some with the crew members on my left. It was the closest thing I had witnessed to a family meal since we had been on board. The food was better, the pace of the meal slower and the conversations more relaxed. After we had all enjoyed chocolate cake a la mode for desert ,Captain Svensson got up and came around the table to where I was still working on the last of my cake and ice cream. "Come on down to my office, please, when you are done, Timm," he said while lightly touching my shoulder.

I told him I would be there in a minute or two, figuring it would not take me much longer to finish my desert.

I finished up my cake and ice cream and excused myself from the table. The captain's office was just down the passageway from the dining room so the walk itself was only a few seconds. I knocked a light double tap polite knock, and Captain Svensson called me in.

"Please have a seat, Timm," Captain Svensson said as he stood behind his desk, and then he sat when I did. I waited for him to begin the conversation.

"I am very concerned about Mylan," he began after a short pause. "At the Merchant Marine Academy we are told stories of men throwing themselves from the ship, committing suicide induced from psychosis."

I stared back at him, not sure what to make of his dramatic imagery. It was immediately clear to me that the Ivan Gorthon's young captain was not joking.

"Captain, I can assure you that would never happen with Mylan. His mental constitution is stronger than anyone I know. He has just been recovering from drinking way too much. He simply overdid it last night, that's all."

The captain's concern seemed way overblown to me, but I had sensed something coming. He had asked about Mylan at every opportunity during the day, after all.

"Well, I know you know your friend way better than I do. And I recognize this concern I have is probably unjustified...and I know you were in the navy, so I am not worried about you. Nevertheless, you need to know, the weather is going to get much worse as we go around Nova Scotia. There is a Nor'easter headed up the Atlantic seaboard and we are going to go right through it."

The captain paused as if he expected me to say something. I realized where he was headed with the conversation and decided to let him continue. "The North Sea in the middle of the winter in a Nor'easter is not something I think Mylan will take kindly to. This is our only stop before we get to Corner Brook. I want you and Mylan to think about getting off the ship tomorrow here in Portland."

I nodded an okay and then asked a question just to be sure I understood our options, "So you are asking us to consider it, you aren't ordering us off your ship?"

"That is right. It is your decision," he confirmed, but then added, "That said, it is my strong suggestion, call it a recommendation, that you do get off – if for no other reason than to avoid what I believe will be very rough seas over at least a full day, maybe two days." Svensson had clearly thought through the issues all day and was fully committed to his view.

I got up from my chair, stepped up to the captain's desk and extended my hand. He stood up and shook hands with me. "You are a compassionate captain and I can tell you have given this a lot of thought. I do understand why you are concerned. I will go talk to Mylan about it. We will let you know before bedtime tonight, Captain."

From the captain's office I went directly to the stateroom. Mylan was at the desk reading.

"How are you feeling now, MD? You just missed the best dinner we will probably get on this ship by the way." I wondered if it might be the last dinner we'd have on the ship.

"My head is clear. I am thinking I will want to have a little something to eat before going to bed, but I am okay with missing that dinner." Mylan stated matter-of-factly, as I knew him to do often.

"That's good to hear, that you are feeling better that is. So we need to make a big decision."

"We do? About what?"

"Captain Svensson asked me to come to his office after dinner. He is really concerned about how bad the weather is probably going to be off of Nova Scotia - the scary North Sea in a Nor'easter in winter."

"So there is a storm coming?" Mylan didn't sound at all enthused.

"Apparently there is. He is strongly recommending that we get off the ship here in Portland. He said it was our decision but that if he were in our shoes he would just as soon miss the heavy seas that will result from the Nor'easter storm out in the North Sea."

Mylan leaned back in the chair at the desk. "Hmm...I kind of feel like going outside for a bit. Let's go up on the observation deck and talk this over."

"All right. Sounds like a plan," I responded, "It is really cold, seriously cold," I added, remembering my last foray into the outdoors, "If you have long johns, I would put them on."

"Okay I will." And with that he got up from the chair and moved over to the bunks where his bag lay on the ground at the pillow end.

"Okay, I am going to put mine on too." I turned to get my long underwear out of my bag in the closet.

When we got up to the observation deck it was even colder, and the frigid air was condensing moisture off the harbor even more dramatically than when the Gorthon had moved to its anchorage position three hours before. The steam rising off the warmer water in the harbor took on a mystical quality. As beautiful and enchanting as it was, the bitterly cold air was what immediately had our attention.

"Holy shit. It is probably 20 degrees colder than it was when we pulled in, Mylan." I gasped as we let the door shut to the charthouse behind us.

"You ain't kidding." Mylan looked around at the city of Portland all around the bay. "Well let's get to discussing this. I am thinking this cold is a good motivator for keeping the talk short."

As the one who had gotten us into the situation I felt compelled to lead off. "Let me just start by saying I am fine with getting off the ship. Honestly, I kind of feel like we have gotten 80-90% of the experience of the ship already. I have been in rough seas before, when I was a midshipman. It is no fun. You know, Mylan, I have never gotten seasick on a ship and I probably wouldn't get sick if we were to stay on the ship and go through the Nor'easter. Given what you have been through over the last 20 hours or so, and this I am pretty sure is the captain's concern, I am worried that you might. You have never experienced it to know how your body would respond. There is no escaping it once we are out there."

Mylan looked around the bay for a while. "What would we do if we get off? Go home?"

"Well, we could rent a car here in Portland and drive up to Newfoundland I suppose. Do you want to head up there? It will obviously cost us some more to do that, hotels, food, the car..." I wanted Mylan to know that I was game for continuing the adventure via a different mode of transportation.

"Is that what you would like to do?"

"It is. We have carved out this time between semesters so why not? We could meet the ship in Corner Brook and we would probably have even more time to see things on Newfoundland than with our original plan," I reasoned, "We would already have a car, after all, so why not use it some to see the island?"

My logic worked. Mylan was in. "Okay. So we get off the ship in the morning; we get a rental car and then head north. Where do we go to get up to Newfoundland anyway?"

My trip to Nova Scotia on my honeymoon and my more recent trip to Newfoundland with my father had prepared me. "The ferry to Newfoundland goes out of North Sydney at the north end of Cape Breton which is at the north end of Nova Scotia. I am just guessing here but I would think it would be around twelve hours or so to drive up there from Portland."

That was enough for Mylan. We had a plan. We would cross the border into Canada by car, and make our way north to Newfoundland by land and by ferry, not by sea and via the Ivan Gorthon. "Let's head back down." He blurted out through chattering teeth. "I have had enough of this frigid cold. Haven't you?"

I had. The cold was so penetrating even in the still night air that I felt we were risking frostbite if we stayed topside much longer. My teeth were chattering too.

Later that evening, I let Captain Svensson know that we would debark in the morning. Getting off the Ivan Gorthon on Saturday meant we would have spent all of three full days on the ship — three days that had felt like at least five.

Chapter 12 – Port Agents, Customs and Drug Sniffing Dogs

The Ivan Gorthon pulled its anchor off the floor of Portland harbor at 7:30 and made its way over to its pier by 8:00am. We were tied up and fully secure by 8:15. The port agent came aboard the ship as soon as the gangway was across the ship and was in the captain's office by 8:30.

Mylan and I had our stuff together and we were preparing to debark when a call went over the public address system on the ship for us to come to the captain's office.

When Mylan and I got to the captain's office Captain Svensson and the port agent were just coming out the door of the office.

"Good morning Captain," I greeted as Mylan and I walked up to the two men. "What's up?"

Captain Svensson did not beat around the bush. "Gentlemen, our port agent here, Mr. Norman, informs me that there are substantial penalties for civilian riders to debark in the United States if they first boarded in the United States."

Mylan's attorney instincts were immediately awakened, "Good morning, Mr. Norman," he began cordially enough, "What law or code applies exactly?" I moved out of the way to let Mylan come in closer.

Mr. Norman was taken off guard slightly but did not back down. "I am not sure what the name of the law is or the code number, but what I know is that a civilian riding a merchant vessel cannot move from one U.S. port to another without documentation, the law is there to deter stowaways."

Mylan responded as if he had been given over an hour to prepare. "First of all we are not stowaways, and no doubt the captain has told you that. Secondly, we are not paying riders under formal paperwork; we are guests of the Gorthon shipping company. Thirdly, our original intent was not to debark here in Portland. We were originally planning on riding the ship to Corner Brook, Newfoundland. The captain has asked us to consider getting off the ship because of foul weather expected over the next few days. We are not trying to pull anything on anyone here."

Mr. Norman was undeterred. "Look, the fines are significant – for you and for the ship. This is not something you want to mess with."

"What kind of fines are you talking about?" I interrupted, "and who is going to fine us and the ship?"

"Several thousand dollars for each of you individually and a similar amount for the ship – probably five or six thousand," Mr. Norman stated as if he had seen the scenario play out before.

"We are not paying any fines and neither is the ship," Mylan interjected, now fully agitated. "We will stay onboard and make the trip to Corner Brook if we have to. I vaguely remember studying this in law school when we studied maritime law. I am fairly sure this law only applies to paying customers and stowaways; we are neither. Who makes this determination anyway, Mr. Norman?"

At this point I believe our port agent realized Mylan was no legal novice and decided to take a different, more accommodating, tact. "Customs would make the determination. I could take you guys over there and see what they say. If they want to press charges or levy a fine you could come back to the ship. If not you could be on your way I would think."

"That's fair," Mylan said, realizing he had won Mr. Norman over to something reasonable, if not completely without risk. "When will you be leaving the ship? We will get our things and join you."

"I have what I need from the captain until later so I'm leaving right now actually. I wasn't planning on going over to Customs but I can drop you there and wait for a bit to see what they say," Mr. Norman replied, taking on a more agreeable tone.

"Well, we are ready to go. We just need to get our things. Can you give us a couple minutes?" Mylan asked.

"Sure. Meet me at the bottom of the gangway. My van is right there. I will run you guys over to Customs. It isn't too far from the pier, actually, only about a mile and half."

"Okay. We will be there in a minute or two," Mylan responded.

Back to the stateroom we went to gather our bags. After a quick visual inspection of the room we turned on our heels and were back down the passageway and off the ship down the gangway. Mr. Norman was on his radio talking to someone when we got to his white van.

"Jump on in guys," Mr. Norman said after finishing his conversation on his Motorola walkie-talkie.

After tossing his bag into the second row seat of the van, Mylan took the shotgun seat and I jumped in the first row passenger seat behind Mr. Norman and Mylan. I was relying on Mylan's legal savvy and his gift for negotiating to get us out of this fix. I had fully re-geared my mind to expect that for this trip we would be traveling by car from this day forward. It really was up to Mylan to make sure we didn't have to go back on the ship and endure the rough seas that were expected off the coast of Nova Scotia.

Mr. Norman put the van into drive and turned the wheel for the van to leave the pier. "So you guys got on the Ivan Gorthon in Richmond, Virginia?"

Mylan took up the conversation while I listened in. "Yes, we got on the ship on Wednesday morning, the 30th of December. As I said when we were talking with the captain, our plan was to ride the ship all the way to Corner Brook."

"Well I don't want you guys to get fined and I don't want the ship to get fined either, so hopefully Customs will listen to your story and let you be on your way."

"I can't see why they would want to fine us or the ship." Mylan replied. "The captain asked us to consider getting off the ship, he isn't ordering us off. I have to believe that Customs knows there is a big Nor'easter storm coming and will understand what is happening. We could just stay on the ship and we will if there are any issues."

Just as the van left the barrier that marked the end of the pier property I looked to the right down the cross street and caught a brief glimpse of a lobster shop. "Hey Mylan, I just saw a lobster shop down that street. If we do get by Customs how about we get some lobsters for the crew?"

Our increasingly friendly driver Mr. Norman jumped in with some information at this point. "Guys, there are several lobster shops around the corner from that place you can see there. You won't have any problem getting some lobster in that area."

Mylan agreed with me. "I think that would be a great idea. I wonder how many we should buy."

"I'm thinking four or five; let's see how much they are and how big they are. Not everybody likes lobster and Miko could just cook it up and make soup or some other dish out of the meat – that will be his issue to worry about."

"Well first we need to get past Customs and then we need to get a car," Mylan reminded me.

"I know. You get us past Customs and we can head out to the airport to rent a car. Once we have the car we can do whatever we want. We probably ought to grab a good lunch before we start driving anyway."

A couple minutes later Mr. Norman parked the van in a spot just outside the front door of the Customs building. The building wasn't that far from another pier on the harbor – one designed for cruise ships. At this time of year there were none of those types of ships anywhere near Portland, Maine. Mylan and I climbed out of the van and grabbed our bags. Mr. Norman accompanied us into the building.

The interior of the Customs building was not unlike that of a medium sized town's bus station – a good deal of open space in the middle with a couple of offices around the back and a couple of windows to talk to the agents on duty. Mr. Norman directed us to the window to the right.

"Good morning Jim," Mr. Norman began, making it clear he was familiar with the Customs agent at the window, "These gentlemen are off of Ivan Gorthon, which just moored at Pier 6 a short time ago. They are guests of the shipping company, not paying riders, not paid crew. The Ivan Gorthon captain has asked them to debark rather than continue onboard due to the bad weather that is anticipated."

The Customs agent took a lengthy look at Mylan and then at me. "Do you guys have identification?" He asked cocking his head to the left some.

"Yes sir," Mylan and I answered together, immediately grabbing for our wallets. Mylan was taking charge now and I was glad he was. Mylan pulled out both his Louisiana driver's license and his University of Virginia Darden ID. I saw what he had done and also pulled my student ID along with my Virginia driver's license. We both handed them over to the Customs agent.

"So one of you tell me why you were on that ship," Customs agent Jim ordered.

"We are simply having an adventure over our Christmas break, officer. Timm's wife works with a guy who does logistics management for their company and he was able to get Gorthon Lines to invite us onto the Ivan Gorthon. We fully intended to ride the ship up to Corner Brook, but the captain has asked us to get off here in Portland." I knew Mylan was keeping it brief on purpose, hoping he wouldn't need to get into any more detail than that.

"What do you have in your bags?" Jim the Customs agent asked coolly.

"Clothes, cameras, toiletries, books, that kind of thing." Mylan responded again, sticking with the short and sweet approach.

Mr. Norman watched the back and forth with keen interest, not sure what was going to happen next.

Jim cocked his head again and looked first at me and then back at Mylan. "Well this is highly unusual but I believe you. But just to be sure I am going to ask you to let our dogs sniff your bags before I let you go. Any problem with that?"

Mylan looked at me just to make sure I didn't have any objections. I shrugged a "why not?" body language response, figuring the less I said the better. Mylan turned back towards Jim. "No problem at all."

Mr. Norman turned to us. "I think you guys are going to be fine. I don't see any reason for me to stick around at this point."

"Any issue from here you won't be able to help us with anyway!" Mylan joked, knowing there shouldn't be any problems with the bags.

"You are right about that." Mr. Norman said and extended his hand to Mylan. "You guys take care of yourselves. You are going to drive north today, right?"

Mylan nodded. "That is the plan. Go get us a rental car first. Buy some lobster, get some food and take off. Thanks for bringing us over here and giving us a chance to get off the ship. I think Captain Svensson will be far more comfortable with us off the ship."

I shook the port agent's hand as well. "Mr. Norman, you had me pretty scared back on the ship. Thanks for not going Gestapo on us. No way we wanted the ship to get a fine on account of us, and we certainly can't afford a big fine. Looks like everything is going to work out okay assuming they don't find anything in our bags...which they shouldn't."

Mr. Norman was just out the door of the Customs building when the German Sheppard drug-sniffing dog was brought out from one of the offices by Customs agent Jim. Jim directed Mylan and me to open our bags and stand back. "Just unzip your bags and stand back to let my dog do his job."

The dog sniffed each bag deliberately but quickly and looked up at Jim as if to say "Is that it? Just a couple bags?" Jim turned to us and said the words we had been waiting to hear, "You are free to go, gentlemen."

Mylan turned to me and said quietly with a big grin, "Well we escaped successfully!"

I couldn't help but take note of Mylan's cool throughout the morning, "Good thing you knew what to say to Mr. Norman. I swear I thought we were in deep shit when we were first getting the situation from Captain Svensson. If it wasn't for you pushing back on the port agent to back up his threats of fines, I doubt we would be over here getting ready to jump in a cab."

"Never know," Mylan humbly acknowledged. "Let's get out of here and see if we can get a cab to the airport."

We zipped up our bags and marched triumphantly out the front door of the Customs building out to the street to flag a taxicab.

Chapter 13 – Rental Cars, Lobster, and Pizza

Mylan and I got to the edge of the sidewalk and looked backwards into the oncoming flow of traffic. A taxi with its light on indicating it was empty and available moved towards us from a couple blocks away. We both raised our right arms to hail the cab. If we were in New York City maybe the cab driver would have missed seeing us. In Portland in January, there was no way he missed us. Sure enough, the taxi rolled up alongside the sidewalk in front of the Customs building to pick us up.

"Looking like our lucky day, MD." I said feeling better with every passing minute. The scare of the morning was still fresh in my mind. Mr. Norman had turned out to be a decent guy even though he had really gotten my heart rate up with his talk of big fines for breaking some obscure law we had no idea existed. Thank God Mylan had jumped in and used his legal background and incredible negotiating skills to turn the tide. The exchange in front of the captain's office had happened just forty minutes earlier but it felt more like fifteen or twenty minutes to me since I had mainly been a passive observer along for the ride.

We crawled into the cab after tossing our bags into the trunk. I took the lead with the cab driver. Mylan had done enough for the morning already. "We want to rent a car. How far to the airport and what other options are there closer by?" I asked the driver, an older Italian American who sat tall in his seat.

"Where are you planning on going with the car?" The driver asked somewhat unexpectedly.

"Up to Canada. Does that matter?" I responded.

"Sure does. I will take you to the airport. The couple places closer don't rent for leaving the country and the airport isn't that far away anyway. You will have lots of choices there."

"I like the airport in any case." Mylan interjected. "When we come back we can drop it there and have the option of taking a flight home."

"Yeah, I agree, although I wonder if we will able to get a flight or if we will want to pay whatever it will cost at this short notice. I guess we will cross that bridge when we get to it." I said thinking ahead to the few days down the road when we would be returning the car.

"We can check with a few of the airlines when we are at the airport before we get the car or before we leave with the car," Mylan suggested, once again one step ahead of me.

"Good idea. That will give us an idea of what we will want to do when we get back into Portland on the way back home. Given that we can't be sure when we will be back in Portland, I don't see how we can book anything."

"No, you are right about that," Mylan concurred, "But we will have the option just in case."

Just as the taxicab was crossing a bridge over a narrow section of the harbor our knowledgeable driver interjected with the customary, and almost always necessary, cab driver question, "Where do you guys want me to drop you off?"

"It's not that big an airport is it?" I asked thinking it hardly would matter what door we walked in.

"No, I don't suppose it is, but I could drop you at the main terminal or I could drop you closer to the rental cars." He had been overhearing the conversation apparently.

Mylan jumped in with our answer. "The main terminal; we want to look at the outbound flights. The rental cars aren't too far from the ticket counters are they?"

"No," the driver answered, "I will drop you in front of the main terminal."

A minute later we were there. I paid the driver ten dollars, which felt like a paltry sum given the threats of fines in the thousands of dollars from earlier in the day. After grabbing our bags we entered the Portland Airport terminal to see what we could see for options to get from Portland to Richmond. There were flights to Boston, New York, Philly, Charlotte, Atlanta, Chicago – all the hub airport cities, no surprises really. The question was how much was a flight through to Richmond, given there was nothing that was direct?

Mylan suggested we split up and research a couple of options each. He took the US Airways and United desks and I took Delta and American. Twenty minutes later we had our answers. On such a short advance time, within a week almost certainly, there was nothing at all reasonably priced. The airlines figured if you were desperate enough to book a flight within a week of when you needed to fly, they had you. In this case we figured we had at least three other options to get from Portland to Richmond – a one way rental car, a bus, or the Amtrak train. It would all depend on the cost, the weather and the time of day. We would cross that bridge when we got to it. There was an adventure to be had still, after all, and it was now time to rent a car so we could make our way northward to Newfoundland.

Mylan was a regular Hertz customer from his days as an attorney back in Louisiana so he led us over to the Hertz counter. In ten minutes we had our car – a small red Ford Escort four-door sedan with front wheel drive. I liked the car. I figured we would get good mileage and have good traction should we need it.

The car was in a parking garage only a few hundred yards from the Hertz counter. Mylan took the wheel and I opened the map of Portland Hertz had supplied. We had already determined our plan of action: we would go back to the pier to tell the guys on the ship that we would see them in Corner Brook, but not before we found a lobster shop to buy four to five decent sized lobsters for Miko to cook up for the Ivan Gorthon crew.

"That corner lobster shop I saw on the way over to Customs isn't too far from the ship, Mylan. Why don't we head over there?" I suggested in a half-way questioning way.

"Works for me," Mylan responded back in his fewer-words-is-best mode.

With me playing navigator a few turns later we arrived at the lobster shop I had seen from Mr. Norman's van. "This is going to be fun Mylan. Come on, let's pick out a couple each," I said like an excited teenager urging a shopping spree.

"What the heck are we going to put them in anyway?" Mylan wondered out loud still sitting in the driver's seat, delaying opening his door a little.

"They will give us something; people don't just carry a bunch of lobsters out of the store in their bare hands. Have faith, MD!"

Mylan finally got out of the car. "You sure they have lobsters this time of year?"

"Oh yeah, you'll see. Come on, man." I knew from my youth living in Connecticut that the lobster shops there had lobsters year around.

We entered the store — a classic small city lobster shop with several tanks on display full of various sized lobsters. The man behind the counter was a mop-haired grizzly bearded 20ish something who looked as if he could just as easily have been in a grunge rock band or be a fisherman just off the lobster boat.

"What can I do for you guys?" He asked politely.

I didn't want to waste any time so I answered quickly and succinctly, "We would like to buy four or five decent-sized lobsters, depending on the price. What's the price for your one-and-half pounders versus the two pounders?"

"The price is basically four bucks a pound so five two pound lobsters would be forty dollars." The grungy young man replied.

"What do you think, MD? Twenty bucks each and we deliver ten pounds of lobster to the ship." I was sold.

"Let's do it. Seems pretty reasonable, actually." Mylan was sold too.

After a few minutes of checking out several of the two pound range lobsters we had five we thought looked good. The bearded merchant put them all into a Styrofoam cooler with rubber bands on all the lobsters' front claws. Mylan and I each pulled a twenty dollar bill from our wallets and handed them to the shopkeeper.

I grabbed the Styrofoam cooler loaded with the five tasty crustaceans. "Let's go. The days are short this time of year, Mylan. Let's get these oversized crawdads over to the ship."

"Who are we going to give the lobster to? Miko? One of the officers?" Mylan wondered out loud as he followed me out the door.

"What do you think?" I asked, holding the door with my back side as he walked past.

"Well, in the interest of time I think we give them to Miko. No long discussion. You can count on that. He will be the one cooking them anyway. Maybe we tell a couple other people just to make sure everybody knows the lobsters are on the ship." Mylan answered, proving again his rapid logical mind.

"Perfect plan if you ask me," I agreed as we approached our little red Ford. "You still driving?"

"I got the key," Mylan answered, showing it to me as he climbed in the car.

I put the cooler in the back seat. "I will bet you that we run into at least two people before we get to the kitchen, and that is assuming that Miko is in the kitchen. If we have to find Miko then it will be more." I enjoyed making predictions and this was a simple one we could have a little fun with.

Mylan started the car and turned to look back before backing out. "How far do you think we get today?" He asked me as he backed the car.

"No idea. But with both of us driving and maybe sleeping a little, I would think we could make it to North Sydney if we wanted to. It will depend on how quickly we get out of Portland, how many times we stop, and the weather."

"Well I am craving pizza so how about we get some pizza before we leave Portland. We could even get enough so that we don't need to stop for dinner."

"You are sharp today my friend," I observed, and boy was it true. Mylan was in a groove. "I like that idea a lot – saving time later with food I love now. You find us the pizza joint and we load up."

It only took us a couple minutes to make it back to the pier from the lobster shack. Mylan parked as close to the ship as possible and within another minute we had climbed the gangway and were back on the Ivan Gorthon.

As we walked into the centerline passageway Henrick Larsson was just coming down the ladder from the level above on the way to his stateroom. There was one person to count against my prediction. He did a double take when he saw us. "You're back already!?" He asked somewhat surprised.

"Only to deliver these five lobsters to Miko so he can cook them up," I told him, "Hope you and the crew will enjoy eating them. If you stop in Maine you have to have lobster."

"Well that is a surprise treat! I will have to tell the captain so he knows we have lobster on the ship." Henrick said as he looked into the Styrofoam container.

"Please do, Henrick." I said looking back as Larsson moved forward and Mylan and I walked on towards the kitchen. "Maybe Miko will cook them for lunch so you guys don't have to wait. And please tell the captain and all the crew that we will see you in Corner Brook. We have a rental car and we will start driving north as soon as we get some pizza somewhere in town."

Henrick replied that he would pass everything on to the captain as he ducked into his stateroom. Mylan and I entered the kitchen with Mylan opening the door in front of me so I could go in carrying the Styrofoam cooler with the five lobsters inside.

I called out as soon as I got past the door, "Miko, Miko – are you in here?"

Miko stepped out of the large storage closet in the kitchen. "I am here." He answered in his hard Polish accent.

"We brought lobster for you to cook for the crew." I said more slowly than I normally spoke hoping it would help Miko to more easily understand.

Miko looked a little puzzled so I lowered the Styrofoam container down on the floor at his feet. "Lobster. Do you know how to cook lobster?"

Miko smiled at us both. "Yes. Boiling."

"Big pot," Mylan interjected, "Boil all five at one time."

Miko nodded. "Yes. Big pot. I boil all five. Don't worry. I cook them."

It was Mylan's and my turn to smile. "Good. Thank you, Miko." We both said in turn.

Knowing that the lobster was in capable and willing hands with Miko and that at least one responsible member of the crew already was aware that the lobsters were on the ship, Mylan and I felt there was no reason to hang around. In the space of a few minutes we had made the delivery. We slid out without seeing another crew member. It really was amazing to me how the crew could just disappear. In any case, the drop was made. I could live with missing the mark on my prediction of seeing two crew members in addition to Miko. Now it was time to find a pizza joint and then hit the road.

Mylan once again took the wheel and I once again grabbed the Hertz map. I quickly looked at it to plan the best route through town so as to find a pizza place that would not be too far out of the way. I recommended High Street to get away from the water and move towards Interstate-295. "Cut north on the first road that looks like a busy street," I said to Mylan as he pulled the car away from the parking lot next to the Ivan Gorthon.

In about two minutes we were at Congress Street, clearly a main thoroughfare through Portland. "Turn right here, MD." I navigated.

No sooner had we turned the corner than we saw Otto's Pizza on the right. Their big sign was impossible to miss. In no mood to waste any time, and very hungry, Mylan pulled right into their parking lot next to their old brick building with large windows.

Otto's was a nice place, fairly upscale for a pizza joint. The waitress came over to our table promptly and we wasted no time in ordering one pizza each — Mylan a simple pepperoni and cheese and mine a mushroom, onion and black olive, my favorite no meat combo.

As we waited for our pizzas to cook we sucked down our soft drink beverages on ice and talked about the drive ahead.

I, wanting to see as much as possible in the daylight hours that remained, tried to convince Mylan to take the coastal road to see a few things as we made our way to the Canadian border. Mylan thought it would be best to just get on the Interstate. The map made our decision an easy one, once we took a good look at it. Interstate-95 went up to Bangor and then made a decidedly northwestern left turn to go away from the ocean. If we stayed on it past Bangor we would be getting further away from Nova Scotia and the province that lay between it and Maine — New Brunswick. We would need to take Route 9 out of Bangor to go east and cross into New Brunswick at St. Stephen.

Once into New Brunswick we would jump on Canada Highway 1 and move close to the coast through St. John, New Brunswick and onto Moncton, New Brunswick before making a right turn on New Brunswick Highway 2 on a more southeastern line towards the New Brunswick-Nova Scotia border. Highway 2 turned into Nova Scotia Route 104 once into Nova Scotia. The first city of any consequence in Nova Scotia was Truro and there we would turn left to head on a more northeastern direction towards New Glasgow, Antigonish and Port Hawkesbury along Nova Scotia Route 104.

We had our route — no arguments there. The question was where we might want to stop along the way. We agreed that if either of us needed to stop to use the bathroom that was an automatic no discussion situation. Stops for food, for drink or for sightseeing would be determined as we went, allowing for some spontaneity.

When the pizza arrived we both dove in as though we hadn't eaten in over a day. For Mylan that was not too far from the truth. The pizzas were large and the pieces were quite filling with ample toppings and a heavy layer of cheese. After downing a couple of his pieces Mylan was ready to get going and asked the waitress for the bill and a box. I followed suit in asking for the check but was able to consume one additional piece before putting my five remaining pieces into the take out box.

We paid our tabs with cash and carried the leftover pizza out in our respective boxes. Our waitress was nice enough to set us up with takeout cups for our drinks as well. We were set for a long drive. It was a little after noon when we got onto I-95. A few minutes later, as Portland faded behind us and the highway began a more rural path, Mylan, driving still, looked into the rear view mirror and quoted one of his favorite Homer Simpson lines "Goodbye Stinktown!"

We both laughed out loud. The timing couldn't have been better. There was nothing wrong with the town, the city from which we were restarting our journey northward. There was certainly no malice towards the very cold port city called Portland we were leaving in the rear view mirror. Mylan was simply a huge Simpsons fan and he couldn't resist. I had a feeling I would be hearing a few more Homer lines as the trip progressed.

Chapter 14 – To Nova Scotia

With Mylan at the wheel and me navigating we zipped north on I-95 just a few miles out of Bangor in the early afternoon of January 2nd. Just a day shy of two weeks from the shortest day of the year, we knew we wouldn't have daylight much beyond 5pm. We had been on the road for about two hours since leaving Portland. As we got closer to Bangor I focused on making sure we took the right exit to get on the road to Calais, Maine, the border town across from St. Stephen, New Brunswick, where we would cross over into Canada.

"We take the Route 9 exit to Calais in six miles, MD," I announced having gotten a good look at a mile marker and doing some quick math.

"Got it," Mylan replied dutifully.

"You want me to drive?"

"No. I am fine," he answered. "And you are a better navigator than me anyway."

I was perfectly content to remain in the passenger seat and let him drive. I really did prefer navigating. "I am fine with you driving as long as you are okay with it."

We had never been on a long trip by car so when Mylan said "I can drive the whole time, really," he surprised me.

Considering that he had driven more than once from Charlottesville to Louisiana and back I realized he was used to long stretches of driving. "Well I might just let you!"

A few minutes later Mylan eased our red Ford Escort over to the right and took the exit off of I-95 onto I-395, a short interstate highway spur that turned into Alternate 1 heading down to Bar Harbor. After we crossed over the Penobscot River that runs through Bangor, Mylan again leaned the wheel over to the right to get onto Route 9 to Calais and New Brunswick.

The road from Bangor to Calais was far more interesting than the interstate. First as South Main Street and then North Main Street, it ran northeast along the Penobscot River for several miles, allowing for a nice view of Bangor's nicer homes along the north side of the river. Then the road turned due east and made a nearly 90 minute run through beautiful wooded land. With modest mountains of around 1,000 feet to the left and decent sized lakes both left and right, the terrain was dotted with few houses; mostly the population was in small towns interspersed at an increasing gap until about an hour past Bangor. About seven miles outside of Calais, Route 9 joined with Route 1 and began a short final run along the border with New Brunswick, separating the United States from Canada. The St. Croix River generally runs southward dividing Maine and New Brunswick, but along this final stretch of our drive in Maine we were headed east and then north to Calais. We looked across the St. Croix River at Canada for the first time on the trip. This certainly wasn't our original plan but in many ways it was far more interesting than being on the ship. We were now far ahead of the ship in getting to Newfoundland, and Mylan was determined to keep it that way.

After a fairly long period of contemplative silence as we both looked across the river into New Brunswick, I had an idea. "Let's stop at the reversing falls in St. John. We can have a look and take a short break, use the restroom, buy whatever. Maybe find a place to change a little money."

Mylan took a moment to think. "All right. How do we know if the falls will be reversing?"

"We don't." I said because I really didn't know. "They do it twice a day. We might get lucky."

Mylan wondered if we had enough daylight left, given we hadn't gotten across the border yet and the skies were already starting to dim. "Is it going to be light out when we get there?"

"It's lit up so we will be able to see the river and the falls regardless," I replied with the knowledge gained from my visit through St. John on my honeymoon nearly nine years prior. "There are some tourist areas near there for shopping, nothing is too far. We ought to be able to do everything in 30 to 45 minutes I would think."

"All right," Mylan agreed. "Hey, make sure I don't forget to ask the agent at the border to stamp my passport."

I was a little amused. "Okay. You know you don't need a passport to get into Canada. They are probably going to look at you a little funny."

"I don't care," Mylan came back, "This is my first time into Canada. I don't think they will have any problem doing it."

"No I don't think they will," I agreed, still smiling a little at the thought of Mylan asking the agent for the stamp.

After a short run through the small town of Calais on its North Street, Mylan drove us onto the bridge crossing over the St. Croix River and up to the border agent window just into St. Stephen, New Brunswick. The customs agent in his early forties took a quick look into the car. "Good afternoon, gentlemen. IDs please. What brings you into Canada?"

"Sightseeing," Mylan told him. "We are headed up to Newfoundland to meet a ship that is coming up from Virginia. It's a long story actually."

"That's fine." The agent responded flatly, not at all interested in the long story. "Not too many folks coming north this time of year for sightseeing."

Mylan decided a little more detail might be in order. "We are students on our Christmas break. We are having an adventure, you could say."

And with that he quickly changed the subject. "Could you stamp my passport?"

"Sure." The agent replied and then asked looking back into the car, "Both of you?"

I leaned down to the left so that I could see the agent better. "No. I don't have one actually."

Mylan regained control of the conversation. "About how far is it to St. John, sir?"

"About an hour." The agent replied.

"Would you happen to have tide information in there?" Mylan asked in hope of answering the question about the reversing falls in St. John.

"No, but you can get that information just ahead in the Welcome Center."

"Thank you, we will stop there." Mylan replied politely as he took back the driver's licenses and his passport from the agent.

Mylan quickly handed the licenses and passport over to me as he drove away from the agent's booth. "Check for the stamp, would you?"

"Sure." I found the stamp in a couple seconds. "Yes it's in there. Date and time, the whole works."

Mylan was satisfied. "Let's jump into the Welcome Center and get the tidal info and hit the restroom." He suggested and I quickly agreed.

It didn't take us more than a couple minutes to locate and grab a copy of the tidal tables pamphlet the border agent had assured us was there and make a pit-stop in the bathroom at the welcome center.

I quickly found the tidal information as Mylan pulled us out of the parking lot. "High Tide at 7:38pm - I gotta think the falls will be reversing when we get there." No sooner had I lifted my head from looking at the tidal information I saw an RBC bank just a block ahead of us. "Hey, let's hit the bank up there and get some Canadian dollars."

We didn't want to take too much time to accomplish all these important little tasks, such as getting some Canadian cash, and this RBC fortunately was still open and not at all busy. We took very little time to go in, get a couple hundred dollars exchanged each, and come out. We had just squeezed in before the bank closed which left us both feeling like the travel luck was on our side.

It took us about an hour to cruise up Canada Highway 1 along the southeast coast of New Brunswick, with several good looks of the Bay of Fundy, before we approached St. John. In order to get a good look at the reversing falls we had to get off Highway 1, a move encouraged by the toll bridge crossing the St. John River on Highway 1. Ah government...a little use of taxing authority and economics to encourage tourism. The signage to get over to the Reversing Falls and the Chelsea Drive Bridge crossing the river over them was obvious, negating the need for a navigator. Again government showing its influencing hand. There were a couple of large parking lots on the south side of the falls on either side of the bridge and a park with some parking on the north side closer to the falls more to the west of the bridge. I could see all these on the excellent map I had picked up in the welcome center. I suggested that we get a quick view from all three vantage points since the parking on the south side was so easy to get to. I figured we could stop, get out, and walk around quickly enough at each stop that we could do all three vantage points in a fairly short amount of time.

We first stopped at the lot just below the bridge which had the best view of the narrow channel right under the bridge. The flow in the channel was definitely from the ocean inland, reversing the normal flow of the St. John River out to the sea. A person viewing the flow without knowing where the ocean was would easily mistake the direction of the ocean given the flow. It was awe inspiring to imagine the amount of water flowing upstream due to the tidal change – the Bay of Fundy backfilling seawater back into Grand Bay, the South Bay and Kennebacasis Bay on the inland side of Saint John.

Not wanting to linger too long, Mylan indicated he had seen enough from vantage point number one. We had spent only four or five minutes there. We jumped back into the car for the short drive over to the parking lot on the other side of the bridge. The view there was not as spectacular as the first and we quickly got back into the car to cross the bridge and get over to the park on the other side of the river with the closer view of the falls.

Within a couple of minutes the red Ford, with us in it, was in the reversing falls park – Fallsview Park – and there we took a few more minutes to walk the shoreline walkways to see the full distance of the falls. It was around 6:30 pm as we trekked along the walkways. Without the lighting the falls would not have been visible. It was not lost on either of us that the Saint John tourism authority knew what they had in this amazing natural attraction.

Somewhat surprisingly there was a drink and hot dog stand in the park and it just seemed right to spend a small chunk of the Canadian money we had put in our pockets back in St. Stephen not much more than an hour before.

We walked over to the stand at the edge of the parking lot and stood off far enough that the guy behind the stand could tell we were figuring out what to order. I looked up at the menu. "We are doing pretty well, don't you think? St. John by 5:30. Out of here in about an hour. I think we have a shot at North Sydney by late tonight."

Mylan moved up to the stand's counter to order. "We have enough pizza don't we? If we don't stop to eat we ought to be able to get to North Sydney by 1am or so, right?"

"Yeah. Almost 6:30 now. Probably about six and half hours or so to go so 1am is about right."

"Well let's get these drinks and hit the road." We both ordered large sodas and got back into the car. The Reversing Falls would be it for St. John.

Back on the road, we were now in the dark except for our own headlights. The sightseeing was over for the day. It was time to cover as much distance as we could. In an hour we had reached Moncton. Highway 1 joined Highway 2 in Sussex about halfway to Moncton. We were knocking out the low numbered highways, the main highways, up front in our drive. From Moncton we turned eastward towards Nova Scotia and within a half hour we had crossed the New Brunswick-Nova Scotia border. We passed through Amherst en route to Truro on Canada Highway 104. We were moving along nicely. At 8pm Atlantic time, with somewhere around five hours remaining for us to get to North Sydney, the pizza was nearly finished and the gas tank was in need of filling. We could make it to Truro, but there we would definitely need to gas up.

Chapter 15 – Whiteout

Just outside of Amherst Mylan relinquished the wheel to me. He had driven all of Maine and all of New Brunswick – about six hours of driving with only one meaningfully long stop to break it up. I would drive as far as I could before giving the wheel back to him. I thought I could probably make it to North Sydney.

Within twenty minutes I noticed a sign for the shortcut route to Pictou, the little town where you could catch a ferry to Prince Edward Island. I recalled how my wife and I had taken the road and the short ferry ride over to the picturesque little island province eight and half years before. "One day we need to go up there and play some golf," I said to Mylan, "PEI is known for its golf courses – kind of the Myrtle Beach of Canada."

Mylan barely acknowledged me. He was focused on making sure we got gas in Truro. "Let's stay on the main road," he said, having familiarized himself with the map. "We do need to get gas and I gotta think Truro will give us a lot better set of options and prices."

"Definitely. I wasn't suggesting we get off of 104." I concurred. "How much further do you think to Truro?"

"About twenty minutes."

In twenty minutes I pulled us into an Esso station in Truro and we both got out to fill the tank. It was a little cold outside but nothing like what we had experienced that night in Portland when the ship was anchored in the harbor. I challenged Mylan to figure out how much we were paying in U.S. dollars on a per gallon basis, a calculation requiring two conversions – liters to gallons and Canadian dollars to U.S. dollars. My father had always asked me to make this calculation every time we filled up on our camping trip back in 1996. It was like I was in 5th grade all over again but it was fun. I never minded doing math problems which is probably why I studied engineering at the academy. Mylan was a math whiz himself so it was not too long before both of us had our answers. The real discussion came down to whose estimate was likely closer and why, something that required a thorough review of each of our thought processes to convince the other who had the closer estimate. Once we had agreed to an estimate that was likely within a 1% margin of error we were able to compare to the price of gas back home. The gasoline, or petrol as it was called there, was about 50% more in Truro than back in Virginia or in Maine. Since this was the first time we had filled the tank we also made a quick calculation of our mileage. With only one filling the first tank of gas appeared to be giving us about 26 miles/gallon, not terrible but not exceptional given the small size of the Ford sedan.

With the fill up pit stop complete we were off again. It was about 9:30 pm. The next town to pass was New Glasgow, a little over a half hour away.

By 10:15 pm we had gotten by New Glasgow, actually around it since it had a bypass, and we were within striking distance of Antigonish, a town I had some familiarity with having stayed there one night on my honeymoon.

Mylan noticed it first. "Is it snowing?"

"Sure is," I responded, not giving it too much thought initially. It was barely noticeable.

After a few seconds of further thought Mylan pondered out loud, "You think this might be the storm the captain of the ship was worried about?"

"Could be," I replied, starting to consider the implications. "The timing matches up." My mind started to process worst case scenarios. "What is the next town?"

"Antigonish," Mylan answered confirming what I already knew, that there was no town of any consequence between New Glasgow and Antigonish.

"Oh yeah. My wife and I stayed there one night on our honeymoon. There are several hotels there. About how far are we from Antigonish?"

"Maybe 30 minutes, if we can keep up this speed." Mylan replied, drawing out the 'if,' realizing the implication of my question.

"Okay. I wonder when the ferry leaves from North Sydney," I pondered. "If we stop in Antigonish we will have at least two hours to drive, probably closer to three, assuming the weather isn't a factor, after we get going in the morning."

"One of the guides I got at the border has the number for the ferry," Mylan replied. "I remember looking at it back when it was still light out. It was a 24/7 info line. I will call it when we get into the room."

"Good plan. I just hope we can get a little sleep." In just a couple more minutes the snow had gone from light flurries to heavy large flakes. It was building up on the road quickly given the cold conditions outside.

Mylan noticed how the snow had intensified. "It's getting pretty heavy out there. Can you see well enough to drive?"

"Yes, I can see the road. But this is getting serious, MD." I slowed down to around 40 miles per hour. "Think we should turn back to New Glasgow or should we keep going?"

"Well we are probably almost halfway to Antigonish," Mylan figured having fixed our position on the map. "How fast are you going now?"

"About 40. Why?"

"If you can keep that speed we should be able to get into Antigonish by about 11:30 or so. I say we keep going but don't drive any faster than feels safe."

"Works for me." I replied wondering if I could keep it at 40 miles per hour.

Five minutes later I was driving 25 miles per hour. The conditions had deteriorated substantially. It was approaching white out conditions and just seeing the road was becoming a challenge. It was better to run with the dim headlights aimed lower to the road rather than the bright headlights pointing straight ahead into the thick snow. I needed to see the definition of the road as best as possible in the blizzard. "I think we are looking at midnight getting to Antigonish at this rate." I said.

"We had better stay on the road and just keep going. We do not want to get stuck out here." Mylan remarked with a slight hint of worry in his voice.

"I can still see the road." I reassured him. "Thank God it is raised a little from the rest of the terrain – that is what is making the difference at this point." I couldn't help but think that it was better for the guy who had grown up in the Midwest, had gone to school in Maryland and lived the last eight years in Virginia to be driving and not the guy from Louisiana. I had had many winters of practice driving in snow in cars of various makes and models. My concern was less with traction and more with visibility. The road was fairly straight and in excellent condition. I just had to make sure it was under the wheels of the car.

By the time we made it to Antigonish our nerves were raw. I had it down to 15 miles per hour over the last ten miles. "Arrive alive," I kept saying to myself. We had seen only one car over the last hour of the drive. Sensible people were not out driving in a whiteout squall. It was a no brainer that we had to stop. We had figured that out in the first few minutes when the snow had gone from barely noticeable to massive flakes that looked almost as big as cotton balls. Neither of us wanted to go any further in the horrific snow storm. We were both grateful to get to Antigonish and civilization.

We pulled into the first hotel we came to, The Antigonish Hotel, which I vaguely remembered was the most expensive and nicest hotel in town. It didn't matter; it was almost 1am. High price be damned, we were fried. The snow storm had taken its toll on our nerves, and we just wanted to stop and sleep. We got a single room with two beds and agreed that we would let ourselves sleep as long as possible, depending on when the ferry left from North Sydney, which, we figured under good conditions was about two-and-a-half hours away. Mylan was determined to get the departure time before calling it a night. He wasn't able to find the pamphlet he thought he had in the car so it was a godsend that the front desk had a pamphlet on the ferry with a phone number. The pamphlet said the number was manned 24/7. Mylan would put it to the test.

After paying with a credit card at the front desk we went back out to the car to park it and get our bags. We were exhausted and frazzled. The pizza boxes were empty. The soda bottles were empty. We weren't hungry; the anxiety of the last couple hours had taken care of that. We would need to grab breakfast in the morning, we knew that, but decided to cross that bridge when we came to it. In a short minute exposed to the blizzard outside the hotel we had snow sticking to our clothes and both of us got back to the room with wet clothes from the melting snow. It was a good thing both of us were athletes growing up and formalities and modesty were never an issue with us. We had stayed over at each other's residences and had shared the stateroom on the ship for several days. As late as it was I brushed my teeth, got undressed, and got in bed in just a few minutes. Mylan stripped off his wet sweatshirt and jeans and jumped on the phone to call the North Sydney ferry terminal.

"Good evening." Mylan began as I listened in on his end of the conversation. "When does the next ferry leave to Newfoundland? Okay, 12:45 pm. Got it. Thank you." Short and sweet. Ideal, given the time. Mylan hung up the phone.

As I lay there in bed I did some quick math. "Sounds like we need to get out of here by 9:30 am or so to give ourselves a little cushion. And that assumes the snow stops and the road is halfway decent in the morning."

"Yeah, that seems right. How about we plan on getting up at 8 o'clock?" Mylan suggested, working in some time for showers and breakfast.

Chapter 16 – We Can Make It

Mylan's travel alarm went off exactly at 8am, and he was pretty quick to shut it off. As he sat up on the edge of his bed, I rolled over and expressed my displeasure with the shortness of the night.

"I think I could sleep a couple more hours. Ouch." I groaned.

Mylan was sympathetic. "It's a wonder we slept at all given how stressed out we were in that whiteout snow storm. Go ahead and sleep a little longer, I will shower first."

"Okay. Good plan." I replied easing deeper into bed. "Wake me up when I can have the bathroom."

Mylan showered quickly and got dressed. I climbed out of bed as soon as he vacated the bathroom and within 15 minutes I was showered and dressed also. At 8:45 we walked into the lobby of the hotel to get breakfast. It was a decent spread with breads, cereals, donuts, eggs, bacon and sausage. I ate heartily a full breakfast of eggs and bacon with toast and donuts, milk and juice. I always got my money's worth when breakfast was included in the price of the hotel room. Mylan leaned more towards cereal but had smaller portions of eggs and sausage as well. By 9:20 we were done with breakfast and headed back to our room. In ten minutes we had gathered our things back into our bags and were out the door.

We figured no less than two hours and twenty minutes to get to the ferry – that minimum time would get us there just before noon. That was the best we could probably do. The woman Mylan talked to at 2am had said the ferry would leave at 12:45. I believed that if we got there twenty minutes before then we would get the car loaded on the ferry to Newfoundland. We were cutting it close and we knew it.

Mylan took the wheel and promised me he would drive safely but pledged to keep up a good pace. Off we went in the still chilly but markedly warmer conditions of the January 3rd morning. The snow from the previous evening was melting fast, but the roads were still slushy getting out of Antigonish. The first part of the drive that morning on Canada Route 104 running eastward toward Port Hastings challenged our schedule and our patience. Getting out of Antigonish meant dealing with the leftovers of the weather we had driven in getting into town. It was warmer than it was in the middle of the night but the snow was just starting to turn to slush. So we were behind schedule right off the bat as the slushy conditions prevented Mylan from putting the pedal to the metal.

About a half-hour into the drive along Route 104, just shy of the Strait of Canso that separated the southern mainland portion of Nova Scotia from the northern islands of Cape Breton, the conditions improved dramatically. It seemed as if the snow storm had largely missed this portion of the road. The road was wet, but no sign of snow melting was apparent. Mylan was able to pick up the speed as we passed over the Strait of Canso Bridge. At this southwestern edge of Cape Breton Island at Port Hastings Mylan felt he could drive in a normal way. I figured we had lost 10-15 minutes off of the minimum time to North Sydney. It was 10:20. It had taken us 50 minutes to go 32 miles.

When we turned onto Route 105 to begin our northeasterly run to North Sydney we were making pretty good time on a dry road surface. Cape Breton Island, really two islands split into a larger northwestern section and smaller southeastern section by Bras d' Or Lake, provided a scenic drive no matter the route taken. We had decided to take Route 105 up the western edge of the lake along Barra Strait until it crossed over the Strait and ran into North Sydney. "MD, I figure we are somewhere between ten and fifteen minutes behind schedule thanks to the crappy road conditions over the first half hour plus," I relayed. "How do you feel about pushing it a little to try to make up for it? I doubt we will see any RCMP up here."

Mylan took a split second to shoot me a smirk. "I will push it whenever the road permits it, if we have a straightaway or some more open road. I don't want to get a ticket up here or risk getting delayed by a Mountie."

"Okay. I still think we can make it in time. We did build in a little slack." I encouraged.

Mylan picked up the pace getting the car up to 60 mph and sometimes faster. Because of blind curves and parts of the road where there was minimal shoulder there were many spots where too aggressive a speed was not possible. The road from Port Hastings to Whycocomagh presented a few sweeping curves but also had a few nice straightaways. Mylan probably averaged around 65 mph over the 32 miles in that section of road. We rolled through Whycocomagh around 10:50. We had maybe made up a minute or two over the stretch. I made a note of the time, "10:50. I think we have an hour and 25 minutes to make the ferry. We can make it."

Mylan put an even more determined look on his face and sat up straighter in the driver's seat. "How far do you think we have from here?"

"Let me add up all these little distances. Give me a minute." I buried myself in the Nova Scotia map we had picked up at the Welcome Center in St. Stephen. After a bit I had the answer. "Just over 60 miles, probably 62 or 63. If you can keep it above 50 mph we should be fine."

We came through Baddeck at 11:20. I was feeling increasingly confident about making it to North Sydney in time to get our car onto the ferry to Newfoundland.

At 12 noon we had just crossed the Barra Strait Bridge after a gorgeous decent along the slope down to the water. The slope coming off the ridge had *the* switchback of the trip, a hard right 180 turn taking us from a northeast track to a southwest track before crossing Bras d' Or Lake at its northern most point. If we hadn't been in such a hurry to make the ferry we would have stopped to take pictures for sure.

"I think we are in good shape, MD. From here we are talking about 15 minutes. We are going to make it." I felt sure after we crossed the bridge.

Mylan put the gas pedal to the mat and climbed the hill away from the bridge over Barra Strait. There was a nice straightaway after we got to the top of the ridge along the Lake, and he got the car up to 75 for at least five or six miles. Then after a hard sweeping right in the road that forced us down to 40 mph for safety's sake, we saw a sign for 60 kph to go through the small town of Bras D'or. I wasn't expecting an American style speed trap at this late stage of our drive. We were almost there so the required slower speed through the little town was about all we could take in the way of patience. Surprisingly the next speed sign said 80 kph, not 100 kph, the maximum speed we had seen most of the way, so the last couple miles were not going to be anywhere near full speed.

We broke over the crest of the ridge separating the Bras d' Or Lake from Sydney Harbor. Sydney Harbor lay before us in full view from at least 200 feet above sea level. I saw it first as I had the luxury of not having to watch the road. I could not believe it.

"The ferry is leaving. I think it must have just pulled away from the pier." I deadpanned incredulously.

"What!?" Mylan slowed the car and took a long hard look for himself. It was clear that the ferry had indeed left the pier. It was backing away turning back further into the harbor before reversing and heading north. "That woman said 12:45! What is it right now? 12:15? 12:20? You have got to be kidding me!" Mylan was steaming mad.

Chapter 17 – "That was just a guess"

Mylan attempted to calm himself as he drove down the hill into the ferry station. He rolled up to the booth at the entrance and rolled his window down to talk to the woman inside. "I called last night and talked to a woman who told me that the ferry left at 12:45." He said in the sternest lawyer voice I had ever heard him use.

"That was just a guess." The woman replied.

"A guess?! Are you kidding me? What is the point of having a departure time if you don't stick to it?" Mylan vented at the woman in the booth.

"I'm sorry. Do you want to get a ticket for the next ferry?" She responded, completely ignoring Mylan's question.

"When is the next ferry?" Mylan had let off just enough steam now to have a calmer conversation but he was still ticked off.

"It leaves at midnight, you can line up at 10pm if you like." She replied with a mixture of sensitivity to our plight and a little humor.

"Yes. We will get a ticket." Mylan replied flatly. "Can you tell me why the ferry left before 12:45? I just don't get it. We drove as fast as we could to get here and we beat the supposed departure time by almost 30 minutes."

"Well, as soon as the ferry is loaded up they go. Most cars have been waiting for at least 30 minutes before they get loaded so that is just the way they keep the ferry from running late. They try to run it a little early." She answered matter-of-factly.

So there it was. Mylan had driven the better part of the way like a bat out of hell only to see the ferry pulling away from the pier just as we had come over the ridge to see Sydney Harbor. It was a sight we would never forget. Now the question was: how to kill a Sunday afternoon in North Sydney...

I leaned over and looked up at the woman in the booth. "Can you tell us where there might be a bar or a restaurant with TVs? We are going to have to kill the rest of the day now."

It was obvious the woman had answered this question before. "I think that the Harbor Hotel has the best dining room in the area. You can eat there and they have televisions. It is a really nice set up. It is over there." She pointed over the top of the car to our 4 o'clock position. "That's it on the top of the ridge there. You can see the windows of the dining room from here. There is a good view of the harbor up there. You will be able to see the ferry come in from there."

"Thank you ma'am." I replied. At least we had a good lead for where to hang out for the next nine hours.

Chapter 18 – An Afternoon of Football

Mylan and I walked into the restaurant at The Harbor Hotel and paused to look it over. With fairly low expectations going in we were both immediately impressed. The restaurant had booths around the outer part of the dining area near the windows and tables of various sizes inside of them in the fairly expansive floor plan. The side of the building facing the harbor did indeed have large windows allowing for a complete view of the harbor. It was a fine set up for a restaurant for sure and there were a few televisions in select spots around the edges and corners of the layout.

The hostess approached us and I immediately spoke up. "Hi. We missed the ferry that just left and now have to wait for the midnight ferry to Newfoundland. We would like to eat, at least once today, maybe twice, and watch American football if that is possible. Can you get the NFL here?"

The young woman responded quickly, "Oh yes, we get all the major US networks and I can promise you that there will be others here that want to watch the games too. Do you have a preference for a table or a booth?"

I considered how long we were likely to be there and asked, "Could we move around some over the day depending on what tables were open? If so I think I would prefer to start out in a booth. You okay with that, MD?" The hostess had no problem with my loose plan and Mylan nodded in approval.

The hostess took us to a booth along the back wall with the windows looking out into Sydney Harbor. There was a television in view almost directly perpendicular to the table. Within a minute she had switched the channel to CBS which was doing the pre-game prior to the first game of the day. It was the first weekend of the NFL playoffs and the Jacksonville Jaguars were hosting the New England Patriots in the first wild card game. The second playoff game was a highly anticipated contest between NFC titans – the Green Bay Packers and the San Francisco 49ers. The first game would take us through the afternoon. The second game would likely get us close to the time we needed to line up for the ferry. With Nova Scotia on Atlantic Time, one hour ahead of Eastern Time, the first game didn't start until 2pm. The pregame program was just getting started.

We had allowed ourselves a healthy breakfast that morning before heading out of Antigonish but with it being just after 1pm both Mylan and I were starting to get hungry. We elected to have a beer or two before ordering our lunch. We figured it didn't make any sense to rush anything, including lunch. We were going to be in the restaurant for quite a while.

Mylan, who had been contemplative and quiet since turning a U-turn in the ferry parking lot, finally let it out, "I just cannot believe how they do business up here! They tell you 12:45 on the phone and leave a half hour earlier. Jesus..."

I felt his frustration and it bothered me too that the ferry had left 30 minutes before its supposed departure time but I figured everything was working out for a reason. That was my Presbyterian upbringing rationalizing events, I knew, but it did allow for a slower heart rate.

I attempted a combination of levity and logic in an attempt to get Mylan to forget about it, "Well it's water under the bridge, or under the ferry or water wherever. It's done and nothing we can do about it now. At this point we might as well enjoy ourselves, watch some football, eat some food, kick back and relax for a while and then get in line as soon as we see cars starting to line up. We will be able to watch all that is going on from here. We could just head down there as soon as we see the ferry come in if we want."

"I know, I know." Mylan conceded. "For the life of me though, when she said 'that was just a guess' I just about started cussing her out."

"I could tell you were angry. And I knew we were screwed." I laughed. "What the woman should have told you last night is that we needed to get here by 11:30 in order to be sure we made that ferry. Had she told you that we would have had to have gotten up at 7am this morning. We would have gotten even less sleep than we did. From a financial perspective this means no hotel tonight, we sleep on the ferry, so we save some bucks. Although we might spend some of them here! Hopefully we can make it to St. John's by tomorrow evening and stay at The Roses Bed & Breakfast. You are gonna love that place. All things considered, I think it isn't such a bad outcome really. If we had made that ferry we would have had to get a hotel in Corner Brook or Deer Lake or somewhere north of Channel-Port-aux-Basques and made the rest of the drive to St. John's tomorrow anyway. And this way we get to watch football! The playoffs! Come on, brother, it doesn't get any better than this!"

"I suppose you have a point on the timing issue. It probably won't make much difference in the end when we get to St. John's. What is there to do there anyway?" Mylan was starting to think ahead and I was glad about that.

"Three things that are absolute musts in my book: fish & chips, Erin's Pub and Cabot Tower on Signal Hill." I said putting three fingers up in the air one by one. "The people there are so friendly, and the scenery is really something. Hopefully we will see an iceberg from Signal Hill in St. John's Bay. They say that the weather in St. John's is mild because of the tempering effect of the ocean, but I am going to predict that it will be pretty cold there. We might be able to go to a hockey game. St. John's is the triple A team for the Toronto Maple Leafs. We will just have to see what the schedule has to offer on that."

"How long are you figuring we stay in St. John's?" Mylan asked me just as our waitress brought our beers.

"The Ivan Gorthon is supposed to get into Corner Brook on Wednesday so I figure we stay in St. John's a full day and then take off for Corner Brook on Wednesday. I am thinking we can drive from St. John's to Corner Brook in around 7 hours if we don't stop. But I figure we will stop a few times, so if we leave St. John's in the morning after a good breakfast we get to Corner Brook in the late afternoon, probably a little after the ship gets in. We can say hello and goodbye to the guys, let them know we made it, ask about how the weather was for them getting there, ask how they liked the lobster, take a few pictures, whatever. Then we can stay in Corner Brook or head down to Channel Port-aux-Basques or whatever you want to do."

"That will give us Thursday to Sunday to get home – that ought to be plenty of time," Mylan replied letting me know he was comfortable with the plan.

The beer was going down easily. We ordered a second round. After both of us had downed a couple Labatt's Blues, we ordered our food. I ordered a big cheeseburger and Mylan got a dinner plate with turkey and potatoes and vegetables. After finishing our lunch we settled in for the afternoon and watched the Jaguars beat the Patriots over several additional Labatt's Blues.

The second game began just after 5:30 Atlantic time. The Green Bay Packers and San Francisco 49ers battled over four hours before the 49ers came out on top. We decided to have a large salad before heading back down the hill to the ferry station to get our rental car up front in line to load.

At 10:15 we stepped out of the car after Mylan pulled us into the lineup for the ferry and went into the ferry waiting area to have a look around. The ferry had gotten in at 8:20 and was fully unloaded by 9:10. We watched the process fairly closely from our table viewing position at The Harbor Hotel restaurant as the Packers-49ers game wound down. We decided to get in line as soon as the game was over because we saw other cars starting to get in line at 8pm. As it turned out the midnight ferry was not nearly as full as the ferry coming from Channel Port-aux-Basques, Newfoundland. I calculated that the ferry left Port-aux-Basques around 12:30. It appeared the twin ferries made two trips a day crossing in the middle of the route. With the trip taking about seven-and-a-half hours that was 15 hours total time on the ocean. The loading and unloading processes took around an hour on each end to add up to 19 hours of total action for the ferry's crew out of the 24 hour day. That gave about two-and-a-half hours between for the ship's crews to turnover and for the ferry to sit quietly at the pier. Having done the math we both felt comfortable being lined up well before 11pm. We figured we had around 45 minutes to check out the terminal waiting area with our vehicle in line and our ears perked up wide open to any announcements.

The terminal building's ground floor had a ticket counter, a security office, a game room, a cafeteria and a TV room waiting area, and the Newfoundland Information Center. We went into the Information Center and picked up a good Newfoundland road map and some information on Corner Brook and St. John's. After having a good look around the lobby, we went out to the patio to have a look at the harbor. After a few minutes there, we decided to head up to the second floor bar to have one last beer before getting loaded onto the ferry.

At 11pm the announcement came over the loudspeaker that loading would start in 5 minutes. Mylan and I were already on our way back to the car. We were about thirty cars back from the beginning of the line. Mylan hopped in the driver seat. I got in on the passenger side.

"I'm definitely going to get a bunk tonight, MD. Twenty dollars Canadian to sleep in a horizontal position seems very fair to me." I commented feeling the effects of the several beers consumed over the long day.

"Me too. I am pooped out and the beer is just making me even more ready to hit the hay."

"Even if we go to sleep pretty soon we still aren't going to get much sleep. Maybe six or so hours." I realized. "Tomorrow we might want to trade off driving some so we can catch up a little before we get into St. John's. At a minimum tomorrow night we have to check out Erin's Pub."

Chapter 19 – Ferry at Night

The largest vehicles were loaded first. That took about ten minutes. There were seven or eight semi-tractor trailers, several RVs and a few commercial box vans. The cars were next. It was hard to say exactly how many cars got loaded after Mylan stopped our red Ford Escort and set the emergency brake. I checked my watch as we got out of the car. It was 11:25, just shy of midnight. Our journey to Newfoundland was in its third mode of transportation, a strange combination of the first two with our rental car loaded onto another kind of ship, a ship meant to carry vehicles and people across an expanse of ocean. This was not the Ivan Gorthon, that was for sure, and it wasn't driving in the car either. We would cover some distance, and sleep while we were doing it, at least we planned to.

We found the hatchway door to the stairs that went above the cargo deck at the bottom of the ship to the main passenger deck. Our first order of business was to find a bathroom; the second was to secure a bunk to sleep in. The signs at the top of the stairs pointed forward to the restrooms. We went in together assuming a large enough facility for several people to use it simultaneously. Somewhat surprisingly, a row of urinals and several stalls were available. The ship was more than well equipped for a surge of new passengers needing to use facilities. Apparently at this late hour more of the newly boarded passengers cared more about finding a good seat or getting a bunk than using the restroom. Then again few of them had likely spent the better part of the day drinking beer and watching football.

After using the bathroom, we found the service desk that assigned the bunks for sleeping over the nearly seven hour journey. We each paid the twenty Canadian dollars and were given a pillow and a blanket and an assignment for a bunk. Only because we were in line together did we get bunks in the same bunk room.

With our bunk assignments in hand, and pillows and blankets under our respective arms, I made my intentions known to Mylan. "I want to check out the bunk room real quick and drop off this blanket and pillow in the bunk, MD, but I am going to stay up until we get into the open ocean. You know me; I want to experience the departure."

"That's cool with me. I am going to see if there is any way I can get a shower before going to bed." He replied as we turned from the service desk and headed towards the bunk room. "You enjoy our departure. Once I get cleaned up I am hitting the sack. We have a good drive to do tomorrow."

"You are right about that," I responded. "I may shower too, I will go with you to figure out if that is doable or not."

We found the bunk room on the next level and dropped off our pillows and blankets. The bunk rooms were built to be quiet and dark. That was obvious as soon as Mylan and I entered the room with nine bunks, three pods of three stacked bunks about three feet wide. One pod left, one right, and one dead ahead. Each had just enough room for a person with wide shoulders to roll over. Each bunk also had a shielded weak light at the top corner of the head of the bunk. The light was on a normal wall switch on the headboard of the bunk. The setup was well thought out. I had been a little worried about the configuration of the bunks having wide shoulders and some issues with snoring. The walls had a padded short carpet like covering that did a great job of absorbing noise. Each bunk had a curtain and the room was very dimly lit. Mylan commented that the designers deserved an A+ for the setup. He was right. Checking my assignment paper, I found that I had a middle bunk. Mylan had drawn a bottom bunk just below mine. As luck would have it we were in the center pod just across from the door to the room. I wondered if the door would make much noise when opened and shut. I tried it out. It was amazingly quiet, not completely silent but without any squeaks or solid-on-solid knocking noise. The padding around the door's seal was fresh and in excellent shape. Once in the bunks we were confident it would be a restful, albeit somewhat short, sleep.

Mylan and I made our way back out of the bunk room and looked around the remainder of the sleeping deck to see what the restrooms had to offer. Sure enough, there were showers in them. They were small and it clearly was first come first serve.

"I am going to go back down to the car and get a few things out of my bag," Mylan said, "Do you want to go with me or would you rather I grab some stuff for you?"

"Hmm." I was taken a little off guard by the question. I had been far more focused on getting topside for the departure than on prepping for sleep. All the beer consumed over the day had probably dulled my thinking some too. I thought for a moment. "I guess I will go down with you – probably a good idea to get a change of clothes for the morning and something to sleep in."

Back down to the car we went. The loading process was over and there were only a couple other people down in the vehicle hold of the ferry. It was 11:55. The ship hadn't gotten underway yet but it was due to cast off its lines to the pier soon. It struck both of us as notable that this time the ferry was not leaving early as it had earlier in the day. I grabbed my toiletries, a towel, a change of underwear and a t-shirt. I figured my pullover sweatshirt was still clean enough to wear the next day. Mylan also grabbed his toiletries as well as a full change of clothes and a towel. Back up the stairs to the main passenger deck and then back up to the bunk room we went. It was a good thing both of us were in decent shape because the stairs we climbed were no walk in the park.

I dropped my things off in the bunk and bid Mylan a good night. "See you in the morning, MD. Goodnight."

"Yeah, get some sleep. Goodnight. Wake me up if I am sleeping too long," Mylan replied.

"I have a feeling that it will be next to impossible to sleep too long, MD. They want everybody off this thing without any hitches. I will bet you they have announcements out the ying-yang as we get close to Port-aux-Basques." I said confidently, even though I had never ridden the ferry. "But I will if it comes to that."

I exited the bunk room and made my way to the upper level indoor observation deck at the bow of the ship. The setup was tremendous. Glass all the way around for a more than 180 degree view. No sooner had I stepped up to the glass to peer out the ship moved. We were underway.

It was a clear night as Marine Atlantic's MV Leif Ericsson ferry departed the North Sydney pier and turned north out of Sydney Harbor. There were lights off the port side coming away from the pier, but soon they diminished and the lights of Sydney off the starboard side dominated the view. I breathed it all in. I was back on the water again. Ah yes, this is the way to travel, I thought to myself.

As the ferry reached open water and the lights from land receded over the horizon behind the ship, I felt myself near the point of collapsing on my feet. It had been a very long day. Forget the shower, I said to myself. Maybe in the morning...

Chapter 20 – Whiteout Redo

Mylan and I had crawled into our bunks on the ferry after midnight after a night of little sleep in Antigonish, so when the captain got on the public address system to announce that we were close to land we were awakened from deep sleep. I barely opened my eyes for the captain's wake up announcement. "Good morning ladies and gentlemen. This is the captain. We will be mooring in Channel-Port-aux-Basque in approximately thirty minutes. We will be making another announcement five minutes before we open the doors to the hold of the ship. Please have all your possessions gathered and proceed in an orderly fashion to your vehicles once we open the doors. Do not start your vehicles until given the go ahead by my crew in the hold."

I wondered if Mylan had been awakened by the announcement at all and craned my head over the edge of my bunk and quietly asked Mylan if he was awake. He was. I whispered down to him "I am going to the bathroom, Mylan. I am going to take a quick shower if I can get a shower. I will be back here in ten to fifteen minutes."

"Okay," he murmured barely comprehensibly. "I will be here."

I climbed down from my bunk and turned on my bunk light, grabbed my towel, toiletries and change of underwear and headed to the bathroom.

By the time I got back to the bunk room, Mylan was dressed and ready to go.

"Do you want to try and grab some food before we head down to the car?" I asked.

"No, let's just grab something on the way when we really get hungry. I am not hungry at all right now." Mylan responded with unusual alacrity.

"Well let's go up and watch the ferry come in then."

"I'm up for that," Mylan replied. "I haven't even been up there yet."

I gathered the rest of my things and the two of us headed up to the forward observation area. There we took a couple open seats. It was just after 7am and still dark outside. The ferry was just coming into view of the Channel-Port-aux-Basques lights and they were not easy to make out. Just then the captain came over the loudspeaker again. "In a couple minutes we will be making the first turn to enter the harbor. You are welcome to assemble at the doors to the hold of the ship. We will open the doors so you can get to your vehicles in approximately five minutes."

"Should we head down?" I asked Mylan.

"Might as well, can't see much up here anyway, still so dark."

We got up from our seats and moved aft to the steps that went back down to the sleeping deck. There were not too many other people on the observation deck, so the traffic going down the first set of stairs was light with only a few people.

The stairs from the sleeping deck down to the main passenger deck had more people. The people from the nicer cabins were getting going and there were a few people from the bunk rooms also just pulling it all together. By the time we got down to the main deck we realized that many of the passengers were experienced at the cross channel journey and had already assembled an orderly line at both the port and starboard doors. The few people who weren't yet lined up were just finishing up breakfast in the cafeteria.

After a few minutes waiting in line, the members of the crew minding the doors got word on their walkie-talkies to let us passengers go to our cars. The procession began and within six to seven minutes we were sitting in the Escort having negotiated the same path to the car as we had just seven hours before.

"Long drive ahead of us, brother. I vote for a good breakfast at some point along the way," I threw out.

"I like the idea. How far to the next town after Port-aux-Basque?" Mylan countered clearly wanting to get some of the nearly 10 hour drive done before stopping.

"Well, Stephenville is about an hour or so up the road. Corner Brook is probably another thirty to forty minutes after that," I replied, looking at our large Newfoundland road map in the eerily quiet confines of the car sitting still in the hold of the ferry. "Do you feel rested? Do you think you will need to sleep some today while we are heading east?"

"Definitely going to give you the wheel today; not sure if I will feel like sleeping at this point. I did sleep pretty well in that bunk actually," Mylan responded.

The ferry settled into the dock with an amazingly gentle lurch, gentle but certainly noticeable. In less than two minutes the ferry doors were opened and the ferry's unloading personnel gave the signal to start engines. Our rental car sat two-thirds of the way back in the inner row so we would be unloaded close to the beginning. Within a minute we could see a car ahead of us start to move and then pull out. Another few moments and it was our turn. Mylan stepped on the gas and moved the car forward through the RVs to our left and the cars to our right. Because it was still dark outside all the cars had their headlights on.

As we first got moving, it was impossible to see what lay ahead other than the cars in front of us. As we moved forward to get off the ferry, the speed seemed a little slow, but Mylan and I didn't think much of it until we got to the opening in the front of the ferry and hit the outside. The reason for the slow exiting speed was immediately obvious once we broke out into the weather outside the ship's protective hull. It was snowing hard and the wind was blowing at least thirty miles-per-hour. It immediately dawned on me that this was probably the same storm we had driven through some 31 hours before on our way into Antigonish, Nova Scotia. I couldn't help but think, "Here we go again." Mylan instantly tensed up and moved up to follow the car ahead of us closely. We were in a tight train of cars moving away from the ferry and towards the terminal exit.

"What do you think we should do?" Mylan asked in a serious tone about 100 yards out of the ferry's belly.

I had already given it a little thought. "Let's head into town and find out what it going on with this weather. Follow the cars ahead of us. I was looking at the map and we can either get on the Trans Canada – Highway 1 – or get on the main road into town that is like an outer road that runs along the highway. Hopefully, we will be able to see the sign to go into town. I don't think we should head out until we know the situation with this snow storm. I don't want a repeat of the other night. I would rather wait it out, maybe get breakfast."

"Hey, here's a sign for High Street," Mylan blurted out as soon as he saw it.

I quickly looked up at the sign. "Take that road. That's the street into town. Let's see if we can pull into a gas station or a convenience store or restaurant or something and get some information on the storm."

"Okay." Mylan leaned forward in the driver's seat at full attention to the poor visibility conditions we found ourselves in once again. Most of the cars in front of us were also taking the road into town.

The procession of cars we found ourselves in moved towards the main part of Channel-Port-aux-Basques. Visibility was poor but we could see well enough to make out buildings as we approached them. After driving a little over a mile, creeping along at 25 mph, I caught a glimpse of an Irving gas station and convenience store just ahead on the right. It sat between High Street and the Trans-Canada Highway and just across from a road going up a hill and into the Grand Bay section of Channel-Port-aux-Basques. "Pull into that Irving station, Mylan, and I will go in and ask about the weather and see what they have for food." Mylan was just as eager to hear about the weather as I, but we agreed it would be best for him to keep the car running and get it fully warmed up. Mylan pulled the car in on the left corner of the building about two parking spots away from the front door to the convenience store. I pulled the latch on the passenger door to open it and leaned into the door with my forearm and elbow. Before I could grab the inside door handle built into the armrest, the door swung open violently caught by a huge gust of wind. The door slammed against the hinge stops nearly tearing it off the car and stayed there in the fully open position. Snow blew inside the car. "Holy shit!" I yelled out, totally taken off guard by the suddenness of the door swinging open out of my control.

Mylan was also taken aback by the door flying open and shaking the car but his concern quickly moved to the snow flying into the car. "Shut the door, man!" he shouted at me.

I quickly realized I had to get out of the car to shut the door. I had to get behind the door to push it shut. The wind continuing to blow on the door was too strong to pull it shut. I pulled my legs out from the inside of the car and put them on the ground outside as I grabbed the top of the door for something to hold on to. As soon as I tried to stand up, my right foot slipped out from under me. The snow continued to blow into the car as I found myself with my lower half under the door and my upper half grasping at the car seat inside the car.

If the snow hadn't been blowing into the car so much, Mylan would have been laughing his head off at me. He wasn't laughing. He was realizing how bad the weather was and how stuck I was half under the car. Clearly the parking lot was slick with ice. "You gotta get out and stand up, Timm. Shut the damn door man!"

I let go of the car seat and allowed my body to lie on its side just outside the open passenger-side car door above my legs. Fully in the snow, I rolled over onto my front on top of the ice and thin layer of snow in the Irving station parking lot. I pulled my legs up so that I was in a crouching position and moved myself into position right in front of the open doorway of the car. I grabbed the floor board rail of the door and got up on my feet while still crouching. I then stood up in the open door of the Ford grabbing the top of the car and the top of the door. I then moved along the top of the door with my hands and slid my feet underneath me feeling the icy pavement under my feet through the layer of snow covering the ice. After getting to the end of the door I felt a little more confident about how much I could depend on my feet for traction. I leaned on the outside of the door and felt for traction as I spread my feet out in lunge fashion behind it. Just getting the door to move back towards the closed position was the hardest part. Once I had it moving the issue was keeping my balance while keeping my hands away from the outer edge of the door. I maintained the lunge posture, one foot forward, one foot back, and grabbed the door handle with my left hand and attempted to hold on to the window rubber at the bottom of the window with the fingers of my right hand. The door resisted at first but the wind had less sail area to work on as I got it moving towards the closed position. I finally got it shut while barely managing to keep my balance behind it. I stood outside the car holding onto the door handle with my left hand and the side view mirror with my right. The wind was howling and the snow was thick in the air. My fingers were going numb. I bent down and motioned for Mylan to roll the window down a crack so I could talk to him.

"Sorry about that, MD," I shouted through the crack in the window of the door I finally had managed to close. "Turn that heater up all the way, brother; melt some of that snow I let in. Anything you want me to get for you in there?"

"I got it on maximum heat already. It's blowing good heat now, we will be all right. Get me some of those little donuts if they have some and a Diet Coke."

I carefully turned around and let go of the car. I shuffled my feet slowly over to the door of the store, opened it and walked in. I made eye contact with the barrel-chested clerk behind the counter and said hello.

He replied in a friendly fashion with a hello of his own. I decided to talk with him right away rather than after I gathered foodstuffs and drinks.

"What do you know about this snow storm, sir?" I asked as I walked up to the checkout counter.

"I know that it just started and it is supposed to last for a few hours. I know that it is moving north slowly." The clerk responded in a matter of fact way that matched his Marine Corp crew cut haircut. It was useful information without a doubt.

I wondered about the road conditions. "Do you know if the roads to the north are as icy as your parking lot?"

"I am not sure, but I doubt it," he replied. "Our parking lot gets icy because the cars smash down the snow under their tires and it turns to ice. The Trans Canada gets plowed regularly after it snows. The bigger issue now is visibility."

"How often do the plows get out there?" I pressed.

"They run them fairly regularly. The guys that drive them live down here actually."

"Hey, thanks for all the info, much appreciated," I finished. "I am going to grab some food and drinks now. I will be right back."

I found some of the packs of donuts and grabbed three plastic wrapped bunches of six in a row – chocolate covered, cinnamon covered and white sugar covered. I also snagged a bag of sunflower seeds, some blueberry pop tarts, a one liter of Mountain Dew for myself and a one liter of Diet Coke for Mylan. I returned to the counter and paid for it all, and with a small paper bag to hold all the food was able to carry everything in my two hands.

When I had shuffled back to the car I motioned for Mylan to again roll down the window of the door on my side. I leaned in carefully and dropped the bag on the passenger side seat. Mylan reached over and grabbed his Coke. I hung on to my Mountain Dew. "Okay, now let me get in the car and keep control of this door in the process. Leave the window open, hopefully that will take some of the wind force off it," I said, hoping I could manage better this time.

I set my feet, again in the lunge position, and opened the car door with the handle on the outside while holding the door by the inside of the window frame. I opened the door deliberately and shifted my feet to the left around the door until my body was up against the car just behind the door. In that position I was able to hold the door firmly, keeping control of it, and not let it open too much until I was ready to lower myself into the seat. By blocking the opening of the door some with my body, I was also able to minimize the amount of snow that got into the car and the amount of wind that hit the inside of the door. I shifted my left hand from the door frame to the seat. I then sat down while maintaining a strong hold on the door with my right hand.

Once I was fully inside the car I reached across with my left hand and grabbed the armrest handle of the door and shifted my right hand to the top of the window. With both hands on the door and my body leveraged in the seat I was able to shut the door without too much difficulty. I quickly rolled up the electric window. What a difference it made just to know what I was up against and give it the respect it deserved. I had never given so much thought to opening and closing a car door in my entire life.

I let out a breath of relief. "Whew, getting out was a little embarrassing, but getting back in…I won the battle. Okay, so the clerk inside said that the storm just got here a little bit ago, it is moving north slowly and it is supposed to last a couple hours. I asked him about road conditions and he said he didn't think the roads would be icy, that they have snow plows running the Trans Canada regularly."

"So what do you want to do?" Mylan responded, not sure what made the most sense given the inputs from the clerk.

"Well visibility is the issue if you ask me. Unless you want to go somewhere to have a big breakfast I think we ought to just wait here until we can see better. We need to be able to see the road for safety's sake. We have our donuts and something to drink. Once we leave Port-aux-Basques there isn't any civilization for about sixty miles — so we need to be committed." I said in all seriousness.

"Yeah, we do need to be committed," Mylan replied with a laugh, recognizing the play on words.

Just as I was opening the white sugar donuts and feeling the warmth of the car's heater on my feet I noticed a flashing yellow light from the corner of my eye and looked up. A snow plow was pulling out from behind the Irving station store building. "Hey, check that out, MD." I said pointing ahead of us to the snow plow just making its way around the back corner of the building.

"I wonder where he is going," Mylan pondered.

"Hey, let's follow him." I said. "If he is going into town, we can follow him in. If he is heading out on the highway, we can follow him at a safe distance. He must know the roads infinitely better than we do regardless."

"Okay. Hold the donuts. I am going to get behind him. We will see where he goes."

The snow plow looped around the gas pumps to the left of the convenience store and waited at the entrance to High Street at the far right of the station lot coming out to the road. Mylan backed up and got behind him with the skill of a race car driver. The plow pulled out and turned to the left. Mylan was right behind him. The plow moved down High Street heading back toward the ferry terminal. Mylan kept at a safe enough distance that permitted both a good look at the truck's rear lights and a clear view of the flashing yellow light on top of the truck's cab. No sooner had the truck gotten up to speed, he turned on his left turn signal and slowed to a stop. A couple of cars went by in the oncoming lane, moving back towards the Irving station, likely the last of the cars coming off the ferry I figured, before the plow made the turn to the left. The road immediately began an upward incline and within a few seconds it was apparent we were crossing over the Trans-Canada Highway just below. On the other side of the overpass the snow plow made another left – this time without stopping. We were heading north. We were getting on the Trans-Canada Highway. Mylan intently stayed in tow behind the plow. It was a good thing we had gotten the donuts, pop tarts and the soda.

Mylan asked me to pass him donuts occasionally as he nursed his Diet Coke over the next two hours. The snow plow moved at 30 to 40 mph through the driving snow storm, shooting snow out to the right the entire way. As we approached the turn for Stephenville I wondered out loud if the snow plow would head into the small town a couple miles west of the highway.

"Whatever he does I am staying behind him," Mylan decided unilaterally. I wholeheartedly agreed anyway.

The turnoff to Stephenville came and passed by as the plow continued north on the Trans-Canada Highway. "Looks like we are going to be behind him a while longer," Mylan noted. "I sure am glad you got that food this morning."

"Yeah, me too," I agreed. "This has got to end at some point. How are you holding up?"

"I am okay," he replied, "When we do get out of this weather you can take over."

"Fine. You have got to be tired of following this guy."

"How much further to Corner Brook?" Mylan wondered. He was starting to feel the strain of following the snow plow. I was too and I wasn't even driving.

"Around 25 miles or so, maybe 45 minutes at this pace."

"He is going a little faster now. We are over 40 mph." Mylan looked at the speedometer.

"That's a promising sign," I replied, feeling a little more optimistic.

A half hour later we were debating whether or not to stop in Corner Brook, should the plow continue on the TCH. It was approaching 11am Newfoundland Time, 30 minutes ahead of Atlantic Time. We decided that if the plow continued on, we would too. The turnoff to Corner Brook was far more tempting than the turnoff for Stephenville. The car still had plenty of gas but we would need to fill up well before St. John's. Lunch could be put off too, thanks to the donuts and pop tarts, but both of us were starting to think about both gas and lunch given the proximity of Newfoundland's second largest population center. The truth was that both of us were ready to take a break from driving behind the snow plow.

The snow plow went by the Corner Brook exit. We were starting to wonder how much further he was going to go before turning around. No snow plow in the USA would be responsible for such a long stretch of road. It was truly remarkable how far he had gone. We were with him all the way.

The highway took a turn eastward at Corner Brook and began to climb the western slope of the most northernmost section of the Appalachian Mountains. The snow was getting even heavier, and the snow plow had to reduce speed to climb and plow at the same time. Mylan pulled us in closer to keep the truck in view and make sure he was staying on the highway pavement. Visibility was deteriorating to the worst it had been all morning. The plow, with our red Ford Escort right behind it, climbed in tandem to the summit.

After around a five minute climb at 25 mph the snow intensity lessened notably. Then, after a couple minutes in the lighter snow, the road leveled off and then the snow stopped entirely. "Hey, we are in the clear!" I exclaimed. The sun shone brightly in the sky above, near its peak of the day, steeply to the south. The contrast in the weather both the snowplow and its tag along partner had endured over the nearly three-hour slog through the snowstorm could not have been more obvious. The snow plow driver pulled his truck over to the right of the Trans-Canada Highway. Mylan pulled us over as well. This breakthrough warranted a picture. Mylan pulled out his camera and so did I. We got out of the car. The snowplow driver saw what was going on with us in his side view mirror and let out a little laugh. He waved out of his window as he pulled back out into the road to make a T-turn to head back the other direction. Mylan snapped a picture of the snowplow and waved a thank you wave to the driver. Then I took a photo as well and waved a second emphatic thank you wave to the driver. As the snowplow headed in the other direction, back into the snow and back down the mountain slope, Mylan couldn't help but observe, "Just another day at work for that guy. Right back into the snowstorm he goes." He paused to let the snowplow fade from view back into the snow behind them to the west. "We, on the other hand, are not working! I am giving you the wheel Timm. Your turn."

I climbed into the driver's seat and grabbed my sunflower seeds. There were still seven to eight hours of driving left, a necessary fill up and at least one stop for lunch along the way.

Chapter 21 – Breakout to St. John's

It was good to have gotten out of the car and felt the warmer weather after the long trudge behind the snowplow. A temperature just above freezing with bright sunshine felt like a pleasant spring day back in Virginia after dealing with the snow over the last few hours. We had endured two stressful snow storms. We were due for nicer weather. With me driving, and Mylan de-stressing, we settled in for the long drive remaining to get to St. John's and plotted the next two requirements for a successful drive across the middle of Newfoundland – a fill up and lunch.

Right when we got going I turned to Mylan and made it clear what I thought of the sacrifice he had made driving since we had gotten off the ferry. "Mylan you have done enough for the whole day. You have given me the easy part of the drive, so just let me drive now and you can try to sleep."

"Well, I am a little tired, but I probably need a few minutes to relax enough to where I can sleep. I will give it a try. How about we get gas in the next town? Once that is accomplished, I am pretty sure I will be able to take a little nap before we get some lunch."

Pasadena was the next town and it was only a few minutes ahead. Mylan grabbed the map and had a good look. "We may have to get off the highway and go through the town to find a gas station. Go ahead and take any exit you see to go into Pasadena."

"Will do. Maybe we can grab some more sodas when we stop too. I need my Mountain Dew."

Within a couple minutes we were in Pasadena. I pulled the car off the Trans-Canada Highway, the TCH, on to Pasadena's Main Street. About half-way through town I pulled us into the local Irving gas station and convenience store. Mylan volunteered to fill the tank, paying with his charge card to conserve Canadian cash, while I went inside to grab a couple more sodas. The temperature outside had gone up at least another ten degrees Fahrenheit just over the few miles we had driven since escaping the snowstorm and getting out from behind the snowplow. It almost felt warm.

"How much longer do you want to wait to get lunch?" I asked Mylan as he came back to the car.

"The donuts were plenty for me for a while. I don't think I will be hungry for a couple more hours really."

"Donuts were good for me too. Of course I had a few more than you did. And I had a couple pop tarts too. If you do get a twinge of hunger, there are a couple more packages of those." I paused and leaned over the roof of the car and then took an extra moment to look up Main Street to the east. "Let's see what is two hours ahead. I know Deer Lake is the next town and it is definitely big enough to have some restaurants. It's only a few miles up the road though. If we are going to go by it we probably are going to have to stop at the next population center after it."

Mylan finished cleaning the windshield and came over to the passenger door. "Let's get going. I will scout out the towns after Deer Lake for possibilities."

With a full tank and fresh cold sodas we climbed back into the car and headed east on Main Street out of Pasadena. In a minute we were back on the TCH.

Mylan decided to partake of a pop tart and have a few sips on his fresh Diet Coke as we traveled north toward Deer Lake. When we got to the turnoff for the island's northern peninsula, Route 430, just before Deer Lake, I was glad Mylan had not yet fallen to sleep so I could point out the significance of the road. "That road goes up to where the Viking settlements are, Gross Morne National Park, and the ferry over to Labrador. My dad and I went up to Gross Morne when we came up in '96. This isn't the time of year to experience the landlocked fiord, obviously. I'm sure it's frozen over, and we won't have time to go up there anyway but...well, if you ever come back up to Newfoundland in the summer, you gotta include that in your visit. Just spectacular. They have a tourist boat in the fiord lake and they take you all the way in to the end of the fiord. Take your camera, beautiful scenery. Well worth it, I promise you."

Mylan, being polite and honest, replied, "I don't know if I will ever come back but if I do I will remember that."

After passing a couple more turnoffs for Deer Lake, Mylan picked up the map. "There's a smaller town ahead in a little less than two hours called Badger, after that there is a cluster of bigger towns – Windsor, Grand Falls and Bishop Falls. There has to be something there. That group of towns is only fifteen to twenty minutes after Badger. We will find something up there. Wake me up by Badger if I fall asleep."

"You got it navigator."

Mylan leaned his head back and reclined the seat some to get a little more comfortable. I kept quiet in hopes that he would get a little more rest. The short night in Antigonish was more to blame for our fatigue than the night on the ferry, but mostly it was the stress Mylan had taken on himself, being the main driver so far on the trip north from Portland. Even though I had taken the final leg before getting to the hotel in Antigonish on our first day of driving, Mylan had done over two-thirds of the driving the first day and all of the hurried drive up to the ferry at North Sydney the next day. To top that off he had endured the stress of following the snowplow for three hours.

In five minutes or so Mylan was out to the world. I was not in the least bit surprised. I thought to myself that if I dialed back on the Mountain

Dew, I might be able to get a short nap myself a little later, assuming Mylan wanted to drive again after lunch.

A good hour before Badger Mylan woke from his forty to fifty minute snooze. "Where are we?" He immediately asked.

"We still have a ways to go before Badger, I can tell you that. I would say we are about halfway or a little better. I didn't want to wake you up so I didn't try to grab the map. Feeling at all hungry yet?"

"I could eat, yeah, not starving, but I will definitely be glad to stop and have something. Kind of fun to have no idea what you might find, don't you think?"

"I totally agree. I hope we find something really local, not Tim Horton's or Subway. A nice sit down restaurant run by a family or something. That would be perfect in my book. I could go for some fish and chips but I kind of want to save that for St. John's. There is a great fish and chips place not too far from The Roses. I just hope it is open this time of year." Mylan was getting more focused after adjusting his seat to a more upright position and taking a hit off his Diet Coke. "Well we have gorged on pizza, we have had a good hot meal and a big salad, and we have shortened our lives with donuts and pop tarts. I am thinking burger."

"Surely we will find a burger joint in one of the towns ahead." I said, indicating that a burger would be fine with me.

"Don't call me Shirley," Mylan replied with a little laugh. Our running joke was alive and well.

We cruised across the northernmost upper section of the TCH and then headed south on the section approaching Badger. The TCH certainly didn't take a straight line course to St. John's from Channel-Port-aux-Basques, and that fact got us thinking about how the road came to be where it was and not somewhere else.

"I sure would like to know the history of the TCH up here in Newfoundland, MD," I mentioned. "Seems to me that this highway is the epitome of a 'connect the population centers while avoiding the mountains and lakes' approach."

"Yeah, there are only six or seven main roads off of the TCH and a few other minor ones to the various fishing villages," Mylan observed, "With the limited population and the tax base that goes with that, it is actually pretty impressive, the quality of the roads they do have up here, especially with the weather."

"But don't you think it is curious that they don't have a southern coastal road?"

"Not really. They have ferries that run all along the southern coast. In the summer you can take the ferry from North Sydney to Argentia closer to St. John's. After all it is about population," Mylan retorted, correct in every respect.

In what seemed like no time we were near Badger. We decided to bypass it as it did not look too promising for a large selection of restaurants. The deciding factor was that the larger cluster of towns ahead was not too much further down the road. Within another fifteen minutes we had arrived in Windsor. We got off the TCH and went into the center of town. There were several choices for lunch but we couldn't find anything that met the local flavor any better than Hiscock's, a burger and fries joint off the town's main drag. It turned out the place was known for its wedge shaped potatoes and its hamburgers. It was exactly what the doctor ordered. We didn't want to take too long to eat but we did want to experience the feel of the restaurant. The building was expanded around what had been a house many years before, and the front entrance retained somewhat of a convenience store feel, although there were plenty of tables in the restaurant portion of the building. By the time we ordered and had had a chance to breathe in all the aromas of the burgers and fries cooking in the back, our mouths were salivating for the food we had ordered. We got our food within a couple minutes and took seats at a table in the front of the building. In twenty minutes or so we had polished off our burgers and wedge fries and drained a large beverage. It was well after 2pm local time when we walked out the door. Hiscock's got thumbs up from both of us. We still had nearly five more hours to go.

Another hour passed and we neared Gander, home of the large international airport. "Let's go look at that airport real quick," Mylan suggested.

"Okay. Sure. Tell me where to turn," I responded, eager for some exploration just off the TCH while we still had some daylight.

"It's past the town, east a few miles. I will be surprised if we can't just take a quick detour right in there and then come right back out," Mylan said playing my favorite game of making a fun little prediction in real time.

Sure enough, there was a road off of the TCH going right into the airport. I took the turn and in three to four minutes we arrived at the terminal. It had the feel of a military airbase with an airfield much larger than the terminal would suggest it should be. A real curiosity, we agreed. We decided to ask more questions about the Gander airport as our trip progressed and we had a chance to talk to some Newfoundlanders about it. St. John's had an airport as well, we knew, so there had to be a reason for two large airports on this island province of only a few hundred thousand people. We would get it figured out before leaving St. John's. We pledged to remind each other to bring it up if any good opportunity presented itself. We also agreed that if we hadn't gotten the answer by the time we left St. John's we would go into the terminal on the way back to Corner Brook in a couple days.

The foray into the Gander International Airport took all of ten minutes, tops, and then we were back on the TCH. Within thirty minutes we were passing Terra Nova National Park and once again I was sharing a story of my prior visit with my father. "We are definitely going to stop here on the way back, Mylan. I want to show you a few of the holes of the golf course from the road. I will try to point them out as we drive by now but we really need to stop and get out of the car for you to appreciate how beautiful this place is. One of the holes goes across a large stream, a small river really. In the summer there are people fishing in it, wading around in it, when you play the hole. The tee-box is up on a little cliff, and the cart path is pretty steep getting down to cross the stream. A signature hole for sure. But there are several other gorgeous holes on the course as well. One I remember vividly has a wide open fairway that is the better portion of the side of a mountain. You drive it down the mountainside and the entire ocean lies below over the view of the green. Actually, I think it is Bonavista Bay that you see. Anyway, it is so beautiful, it is hard to concentrate on playing the game. Gotta play this course one day, brother, just have to get back here for that experience. Hopefully we will have enough time to walk around here on Wednesday."

Mylan was looking at the park and having a hard time seeing what I was talking about. There was snow on much of the golf course we could see from the road. Neither of the holes I was speaking about was visible from the road. "Definitely let's include this as a must stop on the way back. Let's give ourselves at least thirty minutes. If the weather is even warmer, maybe they will let us take a cart out, never know," Mylan said after some contemplation.

In another half hour or so we were approaching Goobies, one of my favorite town names in Newfoundland. "I remember this town because it is the town just before the chicken neck that connects the larger portion of the island of Newfoundland to the Avalon Peninsula." I explained, proud of myself for remembering from my nine-day camping trip with my father two-and-a-half years prior. "If you take the road to the south out of Goobies at the end of the peninsula down there you can take a ferry to France."

"Huh?" Mylan took the bait knowing full well there was a catch.

"Well not really. But there are a couple islands just off the coast of Newfoundland down there that are still part of France. The Miquelons. Look at the map, you'll see. Gotta wonder how that French ownership ended up being preserved. Really wild."

"Interesting geography up here for sure," Mylan concurred as he focused on the map. "I will bet you that Trinity Bay to the north and Placentia Bay to the south aren't more than four or five miles apart near Come By Chance or Arnold's Cove. I wonder if we will be able to see both at any point along the TCH."

"Well let's see. Hopefully we will have enough light when we are on that stretch to see." I realized that the short day was nearing its end and we were still a few minutes from the 'chicken neck' section of land that connected the Avalon Peninsula.

As the sun set, we came across the connector piece of land and despite the trees on both sides of the road, we were easily able to discern the two bays simultaneously out of the car windows on more than one occasion. With nightfall the scenery fell away and we found ourselves on a mostly dark road. There was increasing traffic as we got closer to St. John's but compared to big city highways in the USA it was extremely light by comparison. There were far more cars coming at us than seemed to be going east with us. It dawned on us that the westward traffic was likely the first of the commuters returning to their homes from work. It figured that some people who worked in St. John's lived well outside of the more populated portion of Newfoundland on its far eastern tip.

By 5:30 we had reached Hollyrood and I remembered that it was about an hour outside of downtown St. John's. I also remembered the town just to the north that my father and I had discovered in our jaunt up the northern neck of the Avalon Peninsula. We had stayed at a provincial park campground at the northernmost point of the northern neck to the west of, and on, Conception Bay. On the day after, when driving south to get back to the TCH, we had come upon the small town of Dildo and had gotten gasoline for our car there. "Remember when I told the story of my dad's and my trip and I embarrassed everybody in Speech class when I pointed out on the map the town called Dildo? That little town is only a few miles up that road heading north back there. I remember that guy at the gas station telling me that up there a dildo is the same thing as a dingy, you know a little boat used to get to a bigger boat. And that they call what we call a dildo a didle. Still not convinced that he wasn't just pulling my leg. That conversation will forever be etched into my brain. It's the darndest things you remember in life…"

"Oh I remember. You did embarrass a lot of people with that one, especially the women. Hey do you want me to drive?" Mylan replied.

"Sure. I am ready to hand it back to Mr. Primary Driver." I responded. "I will pull over at the next opportunity."

In another couple miles there was an exit with an obvious return ramp to the TCH. I took the exit, stopped at the sign, pulled through it and pulled over to the right on the on-ramp. We exchanged seats in the car and were off without more than a couple minute's delay in making the transition.

"Do you remember where The Roses is?" Mylan asked as soon as he got us back on the TCH.

"Oh yeah. It is really easy to find and there is plenty of parking right on the road next to it," I replied. "I will tell you where to turn when we get into downtown. It is basically up the hill from the water about five or six blocks. It is in a fairly central location, kind of the center of a wheel spot. I hope we can get in there tonight."

"Me too. It has been a pretty long day. Still want to get fish and chips tonight?"

"I do," I answered. "If we can get into The Roses we will ask the owner to steer us to the best place that is open. I remember the one place about four or five blocks away up the street just around the corner from the B&B. If I tell him where it is hopefully he will be able to say the name of it. If I hear the name I will know if that is the one I remember or not."

"Great. I am not at all hungry at this point. That burger and wedge fries were a real gut bomb," Mylan commented patting his belly.

"I am willing to bet you that if we have an opportunity to take a dump we will be hungry again." I laughed.

"Probably right about that." Mylan chuckled in agreement.

Just past 6:30, Mylan noted the lights of St. John's glowing in the night sky ahead. "Almost there. See the lights up ahead?"

"Yep. I do." I answered. "We will go through the largest suburb of St. John's before we get into St. John's itself. We are just about there actually. It is called Mount Pearl. It is almost as big as Corner Brook, bigger than Windsor, Grand Falls and Bishop Falls all put together. If I remember correctly is has about one fifth the people of St. John's. What I remember about Mount Pearl, and you will be able to see this on the way out Wednesday, if not now, is all the houses visible from the highway — houses that look like they could be in the U.S. somewhere. Very different look and feel from St. John's, which has an older, semi-European, large fishing village city feel to it. Hard to explain really, you will have to see for yourself."

"I will see what I can see on the way in," Mylan replied. "And I will get a good look on Wednesday; you're right. I will let you know my impressions on Wednesday."

I changed the subject to tomorrow's plan just as we were passing through Mount Pearl. "So here's what I am thinking for tomorrow. Stop me at any point."

"All right. Shoot."

"I figure an early bedtime tonight equals a fairly early wake up in the morning," I said, and Mylan nodded in agreement without saying anything, not wanting to stop me from talking. "First thing we do after a good breakfast at The Roses is head up Signal Hill and see the view up there and check out Cabot Tower. Then we head out to Cape Spear, the most eastern point of North America – that's just a place you have to be able to say you've been to, stood on. After that we come back into town and walk everywhere else. We get lunch at Erin's Pub or some other restaurant in town, and that assumes we get the fish and chips tonight. The rest of the day we play by ear with the default of hanging out at Erin's. If the hockey team is in town we go to the game. If not we do something else."

"Works for me," Mylan replied.

Chapter 22 – St. John's

With me navigating and Mylan driving again, I directed us onto Pitt's Memorial Drive, also known as Highway 2, off of the TCH, to swing south and east around Mount Pearl and south under the outer portion of St. John's for about ten miles. Pitt's Memorial Drive ended at New Gower Street as it crossed the Waterford River as it emptied into St. John's Harbor. We made the final mile to The Roses through downtown on New Gower and Duckworth Streets until it got to King's Bridge Road. New Gower became Duckworth running parallel to the waterline of the western side of St. John's harbor. I pointed out to Mylan the important streets to our right, closer to the water: St. John's famous party street, George Street, then Water Street and finally Harbor Drive right on the water's edge.

After the very long day of driving both of us were eager to get into The Rose's Bed & Breakfast where I had stayed with my father a few years before. I directed Mylan when we got to the intersection of Kings Bridge and Duckworth, "Just up the hill and then make a left on Military Road, Mylan, and we are there. The Roses is the second or third of the row houses on the left. We will probably need to pull a U-turn up there to park."

Mylan made the left up Kings Bridge and the left on Military. There it was. The Roses B&B, just as I had remembered it, 9 Military Road, the third house down from the turn. Mylan drove by slowly looking to the left for parking and within another two houses worth of road saw an open spot. He made the U-turn and parallel parked in a quick minute. We got out of the car and stretched briefly before heading to the front door of the B&B. It was open so we walked in.

In the entranceway foyer, The Roses' management kept a guestbook and a buzzer to ring for the caretaker, who, two years earlier, also happened to be the owner. I remembered the routine from staying there in 1996. The B&B had four floors, three upper levels with rooms and a basement with a couple of rooms. In total there were eleven rooms. We held out hope that at this time of year there would not be any problem getting a room. I rang the buzzer. Within just a few seconds a voice came down from the upper floor. "I will be there in just a moment." I immediately recognized the voice. It was Richard, the same owner/operator that was running the place in 1996. Richard came down the stairs, barefooted, but noisily, not at all like a ninja. Close to legally blind, Richard wore glasses, very thick glasses, and his hair was bushy and uncombed. He hadn't changed a bit; he looked exactly as I remembered him.

"Richard," I began, "Any way you remember me from two and a half years ago? I was here with my dad in the summer of '96. We went camping during the middle of the week and stayed here on the front end and back end on the weekends."

Richard's weak eyes brightened behind his thick glasses. "Yes! I do. I remember your dad too. How is he doing?" He asked so sincerely I could hardly believe it.

"Very well. At least the last time I spoke with him. Thanks for asking." I replied. "Hey, do you have a room for Mylan and me for a couple nights?"

"Oh yes. I have several you can chose from. This time of year we are rarely full; although we were for New Year's Eve and New Year's Day. We also have been getting more and more business traffic during the workweek actually — a very good trend," Richard shared, clearly in a good mood. "Would you like to look at a few of the possibilities?"

I looked quickly at Mylan. He nodded a yes with his eyes and head.

"Yes, Richard, we would. Which ones would you like us to look at?"

"How about you check out the red room and the basement and tell me which you prefer. Both of those rooms have two beds." Richard suggested. "The red room is one floor up on the left and the basement obviously is down one floor."

"Mylan, I am okay with either so why don't you decide?" I said. "Same price, Richard?"

Richard replied, "Normally the basement room is another ten loony over the red room, since it has its own bathroom, but since you are a returning guest, I will give it to you guys for the same price."

Mylan let out a little laugh. "I think I like the basement room better already!" He then went down the stairs to the basement to check out the room down there while I chatted with Richard a little more.

"Is John still cooking for you?" I asked remembering the tall and lanky bald-headed cook that had worked there back in the summer of 96.

"No, he decided to move to Calgary. He left last year," Richard reflected. "We worked together for a little over four years actually. He said he was ready for a change of scenery. I cook breakfast some mornings myself and I have a woman cooking for me some days. You guys will get to meet her in the morning. Her name is Teresa. She is very good."

"Terrific." I replied. "Hey, I am trying to remember a place near here where my dad and I had fish and chips, back when we were here a couple years ago. I remember it being down the street a few blocks and then up a hill maybe a block or two. Does that sound like a place you would know Richard?"

"Sounds like Ches's to me," he replied, but then put in a caveat. "There are a bunch of places you can get fish and chips here in town. At this hour probably your best bet is to head down to Water Street and just find a bar or restaurant that is open and serving food."

Mylan came back up the stairs just as Richard finished his suggestion for getting fish and chips in town on a weekday evening in the winter. "I don't need to see the red room. The basement room looks great to me. Seems nice and quiet and private down there. As tired as we are, just being able to get to sleep pretty soon really appeals to me right now."

"Okay, basement room it is." Richard agreed.

I turned to Mylan, "Want to just charge one night to each of us, MD?"

"Yeah. That's easy enough. Richard, do you take plastic?"

"Of course. You guys can just pay me in the morning." Richard was already proving to Mylan what I had told him about the hospitality of the Newfoundlanders. "Go get your bags, get settled and then head out for your dinner. The quicker you get that taken care of, the sooner you can retire for the evening and the sooner you can get going in the morning."

"Roger that!" I responded. "Let's get our bags. I, for one, want to use the bathroom before we head out for fish and chips."

With that Mylan and I were back out the front door of The Roses and back to the car to grab our bags. Five minutes later we were in the basement room getting settled in, using the bathroom and freshening up a little. I changed into a lighter sweatshirt for the walk into town for food. Outside it was comfortably above freezing by my standards at around forty degrees Fahrenheit. By 7:45 we were out the door and on our way by foot into the heart of downtown St. John's via Gower Street.

We had walked a little over a quarter mile on Gower when I felt it was time to climb the hill away from the harbor towards where I remembered the fish and chips restaurant to be. We went up the hill on Freshwater Road, which was at a 45 degree angle to the direction of Gower, not perpendicular. Sure enough, my visual memory had not failed me. Within another few hundred yards was Ches's Fish and Chips. We could see the sign ahead after only a few steps up Freshwater.

Thanks to the time that had gone by since our stop in Windsor, the brisk air, and the fairly short walk, we were hungry again.

Mylan ordered a two piece meal. I ordered a three piece. Both came with fries. The fish was fresh, light and fluffy with a crispy crust and the fries were hot and very well salted. Ketchup bottles were on the tables. It was 8:30 pm and there were only a few other people in the place. We sat at a small table and devoured our meals without saying much of anything except "Now that is good," and "That hits the spot."

By 9:30 we were back at The Roses. We both decided to shower to get the long day in the car grunginess off of us and get as restful a sleep as possible. We agreed to wake by no later than 6:30am. The large beds in the basement room were incredibly comfortable and after the short night on the ferry and the long day of driving both of us were sound asleep within a few minutes of crawling into our respective beds.

At 6am I awoke and climbed out of bed and into the bathroom. Mylan did not stir. When I returned to my bed after relieving myself Mylan was still sound asleep. As if he had a clock in his head he woke just before 6:30. I heard him and let him know I had already been up to use the restroom. Mylan took his turn in the restroom and I got up and got dressed for breakfast. I let Mylan know I was heading up to the kitchen and dining room upstairs for breakfast and would see him up there. Within a few minutes he joined me upstairs for breakfast. We were the first people up for breakfast and Teresa was ready to go with the cooking. She asked each of us what we wanted to eat saying that eggs to order and sausage and bacon were available as well as pancakes and waffles and hash browns. I ordered a mushroom and cheese omelet with hash browns and bacon while Mylan elected to have waffles with sausage. The food was excellent. The chit-chat with Teresa was pleasant, if only superficial. We were ready to do some sightseeing on foot for the first time on the trip and therefore did not dawdle over breakfast. When we had finished our substantial portions and had our fill of juice, we retired to our basement room to get organized for our day.

By 8am we were in the rental car and heading up to Signal Hill. The drive up to Cabot Tower via Signal Hill Road took us just a couple minutes. From The Rose's the route included a one block downhill run toward the harbor on Kings Bridge Road off of Military Road and then a left turn onto Duckworth Road. Duckworth quickly became Signal Hill Road after passing by the big Sheraton Hotel just east of Kings Bridge Road. In a few blocks, after passing a couple other smaller and lesser known hotels and a small group of homes, the climb up the hill took us past the smaller Deadman's Pond and the larger George's Pond, both indentations curiosities of nature carved out of the solid rock that made up Signal Hill.

At the early hour of the Tuesday morning in early January we were the only people parked in the small lot near Cabot Tower except for the park worker manning the tower itself. The wind swirled around the top of the hill. There was ice and snow spotted in various locations all over the large area around the tower where tourists could wander around to see the various views from atop the magnificent entrance to St. John's Harbor. Mylan and I took turns taking pictures of the entrance to the harbor with the lighthouse on the opposite side, the view of St. John's Harbor itself, and the view out to the east into the North Sea. All of the various pictures required walking to the extreme positions around the perimeter of the top of the hill to get the best possible views. On several occasions the footing underneath our feet included snow or ice, or both, and we had to be careful not to fall down. With cameras in hand falling could result in not only embarrassment, but injury, and possibly damage to the cameras each of us was carrying. Both of us walked cautiously down to the viewing deck closest to the opening to the harbor. Mylan was furthest from the deck when I first yelled at him to meet me on it. He had been gazing out to sea from the easternmost point of the area around Cabot Tower while I had been moving from taking pictures of the harbor.

"Hey, MD, you have to get some shots of Cape Spear and the opening to St. John's Harbor," I yelled across the frozen top of Signal Hill and then pointed down to the viewing platform that gave the view to the south. "Meet me over there."

"Okay. Give me a couple minutes. I have to move really slowly. It is very icy over here," he yelled back.

I got to the viewing platform and looked back at Mylan making his way over. He slipped slightly and caught himself with his gloved right hand without falling down. He had put his camera back into its case and had it on a strap around his neck. He grabbed the case with his left hand while he very gracefully found a dry spot with his left foot and held himself up with his hand.

"Impressive balance! You all right?" I shouted out to him when he was not more than sixty feet away from me on the viewing platform.

"Yeah, I'm fine. Sure am glad I brought these heavy gloves. I just wish I had some boots with spikes in the soles," Mylan replied as he steadied himself and got back up on his feet.

After a few more seconds, Mylan made his way over to the viewing deck. He looked down at the harbor entrance and then out at Cape Spear in the distance. "How long to get over to Cape Spear?" He asked. "It looks like it is pretty far away."

"It's probably only a few miles away but to get there you have to take a winding road all the way around, I think it takes about fifteen to twenty minutes, most of that time just to get out of the city to get on the rural road south of the city." I responded remembering when my father and I had gone to Cape Spear a couple of years earlier.

"This really is an amazing spot on this planet of ours," Mylan remarked as he took it all in.

"Told you it was something really special," I replied proudly, happy that he was seeing the beauty of the spectacular vantage point overseeing

St. John's Harbor, the North Sea and the coastline to the southeast down to Cape Spear.

"I wonder if we can get down to that lighthouse."

"I don't see why not, there is a road on the other side of the harbor. Do you want to go down there?" I replied.

"How about we see how we are doing on time after Cape Spear and decide later. We can always drive around the harbor while we are in town," Mylan resolved.

"Good plan," I agreed, "Ready to go into Cabot Tower?"

"Yep. I am. See what they have there for mementos. I feel like buying something."

We walked up the path to the tower gift shop. After a few minutes checking out the clothing for sale I bought a sweatshirt with the Cabot Tower printed on the front for my wife, and Mylan purchased a book on the St. John's area that included incredible photography from every season of the year from every vantage point imaginable on and around Signal Hill and the city of St. John's.

We had spent nearly an hour-and-a-half on Signal Hill walking around gingerly on the icy rocks to look at the views all around and take pictures. After fifteen to twenty minutes in the gift shop inside Cabot Tower it was coming up on 10am when we jumped into the car to head over to Cape Spear.

The drive took us through the city along the same route we had taken to get to The Roses, first along Duckworth Street on the western side of St. John's Harbor and then back onto Pitts Memorial Drive briefly before we exited onto Route 11, Blackhead Drive. Blackhead Drive climbed the eastern back side of St. John's Harbor through a small part of town called Shea Heights before becoming a rural road winding up and down a tundra-like landscape. The drive wound along the top of the ridge line on the back side of St. John's Harbor before dropping down from that ridge line and climbing across four more ridges before it reached the easternmost point of Newfoundland – Cape Spear.

Those who put up the signs at the lonely point of land at the easternmost point of Newfoundland laid claim to its being the easternmost point of North America as well. I found this more than a little curious, since I was pretty sure Greenland was part of North America. Because Greenland is Danish territory and not a part of Canada I could see how easy and convenient it would be to throw the large, sparsely populated island that is Greenland out of the equation altogether.

Mylan and I climbed out of the car and took pictures all around, back towards the north and the inlet to St. John's Harbor, back up the hill behind the tip of Cape Spear to the classic lighthouse, and of course by the sign marking the Cape as the easternmost point of North America. There was no store, no busload of tourists to move around. The parking area itself was not that large, indicating that even at the height of tourist season not many people would be there at once. All things considered, the time of year in particular, it still was remarkable to me that nobody else was there, there on the easternmost point of North America. It was memorable indeed to have that spot on planet Earth all to ourselves.

Having spent less than an hour to finish up Signal Hill, drive over to Cape Spear, and have a look around, Mylan was not yet ready to call it a complete morning of exploring. "I feel like we have Newfoundland all to ourselves today. What else can we see?" He queried after getting back into the car.

I was caught off guard since I had been assuming we would be heading back into town for lunch. "Well what kinds of exploring do you have in mind, MD? How much driving are you willing to do?"

"I don't want to drive too far but I am thinking it would be fun to have lunch somewhere outside the city and see a few more things near the ocean," he replied.

"Well, I would like to check to see if there is a hockey game tonight. The Maple Leafs stadium is a little north of where we are staying. How about we go by there to see if there is a game and then head north to Torbay? That's a good sized little town on the map and I haven't been up there," I suggested.

"Works for me," Mylan replied. It was still before 11am.

The road back into St. John's seemed shorter to me than when we had driven out to Cape Spear, even though it was exactly the same. I figured that was because I was recalibrating for more driving and exploring than I had originally expected. We had accomplished our morning plan with time to spare, and Mylan had an appetite for more exploring. That was fine by me. When we had retraced Blackhead Road back into St. John's, I navigated a back and forth track to get us out to the Trans-Canada Highway, also known in St. John's as the Outer Ring Highway, out to the west and north of St. John's. Once we had gotten to the TCH we headed east to its terminating point at the intersection with Route 40, also known as Portugal Cove Road.

"Should we head over to Portugal Cove and then up to Torbay, or should we go by the hockey stadium now?" I asked, still not sure how important it was to him to know about the possibility of attending a hockey game.

"I am starting to think about lunch a little," Mylan responded. "Why don't we just check on the hockey game when we get back into town later?"

"That's totally fine by me," I replied. "Take a left at Portugal Cove Road at the end of the TCH then. Let's head over there and see what there is to see."

Portugal Cove Road took us by St. John's Airport, reminding us of the discussion about Gander's airport the day before. We agreed to make sure and ask our questions about the two airports later in the day back in St. John's. After the airport, the road traveled past Windsor Lake, a natural inland lake, before dumping into the town of Portugal Cove-St. Philip's. It was becoming clearer to us that the distances to the suburbs of St. John's were not that far. We did not see a restaurant along the road coming into Portugal Cove but we did see a sign for the ferry over to Bell Island, an island that was in clear view once we dropped down off the ridge after Windsor Lake. We considered crossing over to Bell Island briefly and then dismissed the idea. I decided to commemorate the possibility of taking the ferry to Bell Island by taking a picture of the car in front of the sign on the road.

Mylan turned the driving duties over to me after I took the picture and we decided to head up to Torbay to get lunch, rather than explore Portugal Cove-St. Phillips. It was a fairly short drive back along Portugal Cove Road and then to the northeast on Indian Meal Line Road, no more than five miles altogether, to get into Torbay, a lovely town next to a bay called Tor Bay. Driving along the main road around the bay we found a chicken and tater restaurant called Mary Brown's. It overlooked Tor Bay with a beautiful view. I picked up the menu at the door to get an idea of what options they had for food. My eyes were drawn to a blocked out bit of text on the back that talked about the restaurant's origins. I was shocked to read that the restaurant had its beginnings in a Richmond, Virginia restaurant called the Golden Skillet. "What a small world!" I exclaimed after reading the history on the menu. "Can you believe we are way up here in Torbay, Newfoundland and we run into a link back to Virginia just by chance?"

Mylan laughed and shook his head. "And to think we just came up here for the halibut!" It was an easy joke but it really got me laughing.

"No, we're here for chicken apparently. We had fish last night." I sputtered between laughing.

It was a lighthearted moment, and it made us realize that we were back in top form, well rested again after two tough days, and enjoying our trip. We ordered the fried chicken Mary Brown's was known for, and tater wedges, once again. The prevalence of potatoes in the restaurants we had eaten at over the last few days, whether they be called 'chips' with the fish or 'tater wedges' with burgers or chicken, reminded me of the influence of the Irish in Newfoundland. Our food was ready in fairly short order. We took it over to a table near a window so we could look out at the bay. It was a little chilly outside, but compared to the frigid conditions the first night in Portland, Maine, or the whiteout snowstorms we had encountered outside of Antigonish, Nova Scotia and Channel-Port-aux-Basques, the weather seemed incredibly mild. It was January 5th. We had been underway on a ship or ferry or driving in a car for nearly a week. All of a sudden it struck me that this Tuesday was the middle day of our trip, at least from a destination perspective. We had the remainder of the week to get back home to Virginia and that journey back would start the next morning.

"You do realize that after today we are officially on the way home," I said as a half-question, half statement.

Mylan paused to chew and reflect as he looked out the window. "Yeah, I suppose you are right. What a crazy trip it has turned out to be. It will be fun to see the looks on the guys' faces when we meet them in Corner Brook. I will bet you most of them don't expect to see us again."

"I will bet you that George and Captain Svensson and Henrick Larsson will not be surprised. Everybody else I wouldn't want to bet on." I swallowed a delicious bite of a drumstick.

"Those would be the guys I would say are most likely to expect us. That said, I still think they will be surprised," Mylan countered, making it clear he wasn't really interested in betting.

I realized we pretty much agreed and decided to change the subject. "So do you want to see a hockey game tonight if they are in town?"

"Sure," Mylan answered quickly. "What if they aren't?"

"Well given that it's a Tuesday night in the middle of the winter I don't expect downtown to be rocking tonight, but we could check out the bars on Water Street and George Street. We could do that after we check on the scene at Erin's Pub this afternoon too."

"Let's play it by ear, see how we feel as the day progresses," Mylan answered.

"Agreed. Hey, want to head up to the point north of here before we head back to St. John's?" I suddenly thought out loud.

"How long do you think that will take?" Mylan shot back.

"I don't know, maybe an hour or so? Does it matter much really? We see some more scenery or we go back and drink some Guinness at Erin's. I can go either way," I replied laying it out in the simplest terms I knew.

"Let's drive," Mylan said without hesitation, "I may never come back here again."

We finished up our fried chicken and taters, hit the restrooms and got back into the car. The road north out of Torbay took us through the small town of Flatrock and then up to Pouch Cove. The main road, Route 20, continued north to the point of land at the northeastern tip of Conception Bay. The road had not been traveled much as was evident by the snow and ice that remained along its sides, but it was still passable. We decided to make the two-mile additional run to the end of the road.

It was well worth it. The solitude matched what we had experienced at Cape Spear. The view of the ocean and the land in the distance due north at Grates Point, the northernmost point of the Avalon Peninsula, was worthy of several hours on the rocks with camera snapping away. But by the time we had taken pictures and admired the view for several minutes we realized that the daylight portion of the day was more than half over. We decided it was time to head back to St. John's. After lunch and some fresh air, drinking some beer was starting to sound pretty good.

The drive back to town and the hockey stadium took less than a half hour. We found out the Maple Leafs were playing with the game starting at 7:30. We bought our tickets and drove on to park the car back at The Roses B&B. Rather than leave our cameras in the car we took them back to our room in the basement. Once we made that drop off we promptly turned heel and headed down the hill to Erin's Pub on foot. Erin's Pub was the place I had fallen in love with when I was in St. John's with my father in the summer of 1996.

At 3pm on that Tuesday afternoon Erin's Pub was fairly quiet, certainly compared with when I had last been there on a Saturday in the summertime. Mylan and I decided to sit at the bar and see if the bartender was in a talkative mood.

"Two Guinness drafts," I said holding up two fingers just high enough for the bartender to see.

"You got it," he replied.

Mylan looked around the room. "I can see this place full of people."

"Well we probably won't see it that way," I replied, "But let me ask what is on the schedule for tonight here."

The bartender returned with two large frozen mugs full of dark Guinness still releasing the carbon dioxide bubbles down the inside of the glass and set them down in front of us. "Hey what's your name, Mr. Bartender?" I asked genteelly, "I have a couple questions for you."

"My name is Roy. What are your questions?" Roy the bartender replied in as friendly a way as you would have expected had he owned the place.

"Roy, my name is Timm," I said, extending my hand for a handshake. Roy reached over to shake my hand. "And my buddy here is Mylan." Mylan and Roy shook hands too. "First question: Is there anything going on here later tonight? Any live music?"

Roy perked up even more. "Actually tonight after about 9pm a bunch of guys are coming in to play together to practice. They play Irish tunes – fiddles, the works. These guys are really good and when they practice, it is pretty fun to watch and to listen. You guys will enjoy it."

"We are going to the hockey game tonight. It starts at 7:30, probably won't be over until 10 or so," I replied, wondering how late the musicians would keep practicing.

"Well no promises but I would be willing to bet that they will still be playing up until at least 11, probably as late as midnight. You guys will see and feel a very different energy level in here than what we have now," Roy replied. "You said you had a few questions?"

"I am hearing you on these musicians sticking around later tonight. I think it is highly likely we'll come back later for that. Next question: What is the story with Gander airport and St. John's airport? Does Newfoundland really need both?"

Roy pulled up a bar stool that was hidden somewhat behind the bar and sat down. "Gander still gets used for stopovers, refueling stops for long distance flights from California to Europe, from Western Canada to Europe, and there are a few short hop flights that connect more remote portions of the Maritimes also. Those flights are less regular but the airport is more centrally located in some respects so it makes a lot of sense to fly to Labrador or to northern Quebec out of Gander. The airport also has a lot of freight going in and out of it. St. John's is your hub for flights to Halifax, Toronto, Ottawa and other bigger cities in Canada but it has flights to Europe and to the smaller provincial cities too. There is some redundancy. If it weren't a strategic location for the military and for freight, it might not stay open. St. John's could probably handle the additional traffic but most people here are glad it doesn't have to."

"Wow," Mylan said, looking at Roy and then at me. "I think that is about as complete an answer as I could have ever expected. How does the military use it?"

"There are reserve units out of there now, and a few search and rescue detachments and squadrons from a whole host of NATO countries train out of Gander from time to time," Roy replied, "but you know, during World War II that was a huge base. At one time there were 15,000 people stationed there between the RCAF, the UKAF and the USAF. The airport is a national treasure I guess you could say. St. John's is simply a commercial hub. There just isn't the history with it."

"Roy, you are incredibly knowledgeable on the airports. What else are you an expert on?" I asked.

"Music. The St. John's downtown and nightlife. That kind of thing mostly."

"You ever heard of Fur Packed Action?" I asked to see if Roy was the real deal.

"Of course. Three man band. Jody Richardson fronting, Geoff Younghusband on base and Barry Newhook on drums. Those guys are very well known around here. Probably the best known band from St. John's," Roy responded proving himself nicely.

"I picked up their album The Dull Thud of Fur when I was here a couple years ago. I love that album, totally irreverent, and a few of the songs really rock, especially Fur Packed Anthem, the namesake song. I would pay to see those guys if I ever got a chance."

"They do perform now and then here in St. John's," Roy replied. "They have a lot of creative energy and need separate outlets to do what each of the band members wants to do. Some rumors they are going to break up. Wouldn't surprise me if they do, actually."

I took a long drink from my cold mug of Guinness. "That's the only band I know from around here. Are there any other good rock or punk bands playing in town this time of year or is winter not a big season for music on Water and George Street?"

"Oh yeah," Roy started, "We have several young bands. St. John's is a hotbed for music, given our population. A lot of the pubs and bars have live music on the weekends. You probably wouldn't find too much tonight since it is a weekday. If you really want to be here when things are rocking then come for St. Patrick's. We go all week over St. Paddy's Day."

"Maybe next time I come up here it will be for St. Patrick's. I would like to witness all that rocking. Speaking of rocking, are the Maple Leafs games well attended?" I asked changing course.

Roy pulled up from leaning forward on his stool and got up. "You'll see since you are going tonight. They are and you will see." Roy then left the bar and went back into the kitchen.

"Now that is a friendly bartender, and knowledgeable," Mylan noted between swallows on his Guinness.

"Sure is. People are so incredibly friendly up here. That is why I love it up here so much." I agreed. "That and the scenery...and the weather. I should buy a place up here for the summers at some point. I could definitely retreat to St. John's for June, July & August. I wonder what kind of gardens they can grow up here," I pondered trailing off. Then I remembered I had suggested we walk around to see the other restaurants and pubs on Water and George Streets. "Hey, Mylan, do you want to walk around downtown or just hang out here?"

"Let's hang out here a little longer. Since we had that big chicken and tater lunch I don't see us eating before we go to the hockey game. How about we move over to a table and kick back for a bit?" he suggested.

"Yeah, good call. How about over there?" I said pointing to a table not too far from a small stage where the musicians undoubtedly would be later that evening.

"That's fine."

We spent another hour and a half at Erin's before deciding to walk around the downtown nightlife area. It was nice just to sit and drink and talk a little between treks in the car. A few people were in and out of the pub over that period but it remained fairly quiet up until we left. Having consumed a couple of additional 20-ounce mugs of Guinness at our table, we each visited the restroom before we paid Roy and went out into the fresh cool late afternoon air of St. John's.

We walked for over an hour and saw most of the downtown bars on Water and George Street. We went into a couple of them briefly to get a better idea of the inside space. It was a little before 6pm when Mylan suggested we head back to The Roses to take a little nap before heading over to see the St. John's Maple Leafs play the Hamilton Bulldogs. In ten minutes we were back at The Roses, and in five more we were asleep. The few beers from our time at Erin's Pub combined with a healthy dose of fresh chilly air from walking around were enough to temporarily shut us down.

At 7pm Mylan's travel alarm went off. We awoke from our short but helpful naps. Mylan got up from bed first and prodded me to get up too. "Let's go, compadre. There is more beer waiting for you at the hockey game!"

I sat up and wiped my eyes before grabbing my glasses off the table next to my bed. "I am starting to get a little hungry now. Should be interesting to see what they have for eats at the game. And I will have a beer with whatever I get at the game. I just hope the arena prices aren't too crazy high."

"Do you want to drive?" Mylan asked.

"Sure, no problem. It isn't very far. We could walk actually. Memorial Stadium can't be more than a half mile from here. That's exactly my type of assignment."

Another visit to the bathroom and a quick splash of water on our faces and we were out the door and on our way over to Memorial Stadium – the Maple Leafs arena just north on King's Bridge Road.

We arrived at the arena parking lot just a few minutes before game time. We were able to park our car in the extensive lot outside the arena within a two or three minute walk to the door. There were still a few people arriving at the game when we got there, but once we got inside we realized that most of the people had been there for a while. The St. John's hockey fans clearly liked to watch the players warm up and liked to get settled in before the referee dropped the puck to start play. It turned out that our seats were high up in the 4,000-seat arena, which was bigger than what I had anticipated, so we decided to walk to the arena end at mid-level where there was a restaurant/bar complex. No better place than that to see about getting something to eat and a beer to drink.

It turned out that the view from the restaurant/bar was excellent, and there was a table right at the Plexiglas at the edge of the viewing area. I ordered a cheeseburger and a beer, and Mylan ordered fish and chips and a beer. We sat at the table right next to the Plexiglas for the entire first period and took in the first third of a well-played game with St. John's leading 2-1 at the end of the period. At one point the puck came screaming up toward the Plexiglas just in front of us and our table and bounced off the pane with a loud crash. Even though we knew we were protected human nature took over and both of recoiled from the puck as if it could have come right through the Plexiglas. Luckily neither of us spilled his beer and both of us had finished our meals when that puck came up to our position at the table. Sitting behind the net had its advantages; certainly the view of the action was excellent. But it had at least one disadvantage. We had experienced that one.

After the first period we decided to sit in our assigned seats high up in the top level and not too far off of St. John's offensive blue line for the second period. Our decision turned out to be a very good one, as the Maple Leafs scored four times to take a 6-3 lead going into the final period. We got a good look at all four goals. As I expected, and had predicted to Mylan, the second period brought a couple of fights to the ice. And, as I also all but guaranteed, because it seemed to be the case everywhere in North America, the fans loved them.

After the second period was over I turned to Mylan. "Seen enough hockey? Experienced enough of Canada's game? Maple Leafs appear to have this one in hand."

Mylan looked around the arena as if to take it all in one last time. "Yeah, this has been fun. I think I would rather listen to some guys practice their Irish music at this point. Let's go. Last night in St. John's."

We made our way out of the arena and out to our car. The weather outside was noticeably colder at the later hour, now about 9:30pm, but still not frigid. The winter coats we had brought with us, ski jackets meant for protecting a skier coming down a slope at high speeds, were doing the job of keeping us warm when we were outdoors quite nicely. We decided to take the car down to Erin's, hoping that finding a parking spot would not be too difficult. Erin's was only a few minutes' walk from The Roses so if the parking turned out to be a problem, we figured we could just drive back up the hill and park and walk back down to the pub. It turned out to not be an issue. We were able to park just across from Erin's front door.

Mylan and I walked into Erin's and entered into a completely different scene from the one we'd left a few hours earlier. Most all the tables were filled and there was a palpable energy in the place, a buzz of talking and laughter. The musicians were talking with each other and drinking, apparently taking a break from their practice jam session. Mylan walked toward the bar. I followed. Roy was still working. Mylan caught his eye and held up two fingers and mouthed the word 'Guinness' at Roy. Just then the musicians started playing. The din of background talking gave way to the music, an old Irish standard "Rocky Road to Dublin" with two men fiddling and another playing drums. The music was transporting – I immediately felt as if I were in Ireland. Mylan exchanged cash with Roy for the mugs of Guinness and turned to face me and the musicians. I was watching the musicians intently when Mylan tapped me to take my beer from him.

"Thanks, MD." I shouted at him over the music. "I got the next one."

It was a good thing we had gotten some Canadian money in St. Stephen because we had found several occasions to use it. The prices for beer in St. John's, at least at Erin's Pub, made us happy to be in Canada using their Canadian dollars. The equivalent price for the 20-ounce glasses of Guinness in U.S. dollars was under $2, a fantastic deal by any measure against almost any U.S. bar.

I had eyeballed a couple of seats while waiting for Mylan to come back from the bar. I motioned Mylan to follow me over to the far corner, away from the musicians. Once we got to the small table and got a seat, we sat back to listen to the guys play. The musicians continued with Irish standards, one after the other, for about an hour before they decided to take another break. At the break Mylan and I decided to call it a night in order to get a good start the next day. The short drive from where we had parked across the street from Erin's to The Roses took us no more than two minutes, most of which was taken maneuvering out of and into the parking spaces.

It had been a very full day in and around St. John's. We had had the full morning of sightseeing to points east and north, a tasty lunch overlooking a beautiful bay, an afternoon of drinking beer at Erin's Pub and a walking tour to see the nightlife area of St. John's, a professional hockey game and then some live Irish music and another beer back at Erin's Pub. Even with the benefit of our nap, we were exhausted. But we had done what we had set out to do – experience as much of St. John's and what was around it as we possibly could in a day's time.

Chapter 23 – Heading West and a Stop at Terra Nova

After the long day in and around St. John's we decided not to set an alarm for the Wednesday morning. Wednesday marked day one of our trip back toward home. Making it to the easternmost large city in North America was not the end of our journey by any means, but geographically it obviously was the point on the map where we necessarily had to turn around. Our Christmas and New Year's break from school was winding down with school set to restart on Monday of the next week. That gave us five days to negotiate the return trip, this time, except for the ferry back to Nova Scotia, without a ship segment as part of the mix. We knew the road back to Portland via our rental car was the first phase. What came after Portland was yet to be determined. On the road back to Portland I wanted to show Mylan the golf course at Terra Nova, at least the couple holes that could be seen from the highway. And, to complete the adventure we had started by getting on the Ivan Gorthon six days ago, we had to meet the ship in Corner Brook and say our proper goodbyes to the men of the ship.

Mylan and I woke up after 8am. We got the day off to a late start but we needed the sleep before we set off for Corner Brook. We had had a pretty late night and Corner Brook was about a seven hour drive west on the TCH. We took turns showering, got dressed and packed up to leave. With everything ready to go, we proceeded up to the top floor of The Roses for breakfast, cooked by the owner Richard himself. Because Richard hadn't yet collected from us, thanks mainly to the limited amount of time we had spent at The Roses during our time in St. John's, we paid for the two night stay before consuming our big breakfast. Richard put on a serious breakfast for our last meal in St. John's with biscuits and gravy, scrambled eggs and an amazingly fresh fruit bowl mix. When we had gotten our fill, we said our goodbyes to Richard, thanked him for putting us up on such short notice and got on the road.

I took the wheel for the two hour drive off the Avalon Peninsula over to Terra Nova National Park on Bonavista Bay.

At Terra Nova I pulled the car over at the point in the road where the 10th hole tee-box was no more than 100 feet from the highway. I remembered the course from my trip in '96 with my father. The Terra Nova course was the reason I had brought my golf clubs on that trip. We got out of the car and I pointed out the tee-box and the fairway up to the green. Number 10 was a pretty hole, even in the winter covered with a thin layer of snow, but it was not the prettiest. I remembered the gorgeous 1st hole falling from tee to green toward the ocean and several others with tremendous views. But with the limited time we had, we decided not to spend more than a short stop on the golf course. We decided to make an abbreviated stop, and check out a couple holes on foot, rather than attempt to get a golf cart and tour the entire course.

We had considered the golf cart idea when we had come by the course on the way to St. John's but with snow covering the course the weather was not agreeable and, had we taken the time, we would not have gotten to Corner Brook before dark. So we took a couple minutes to look at number 10 from the tee box and then we got back in the car to move down the TCH a few hundred yards to look at one other hole. The only other hole I really wanted Mylan to see was the signature par 3 that crossed the large creek and had its tee box high up on the ridge above the creek and the green across it. This was hole number 8. For that view we had to leave the car and walk down a couple fairways to get to the green. From the green we walked up to the tee-box to see the view from there. The walk took us nearly twenty minutes, but it allowed Mylan to see a couple other holes on the way. The view from number 8 tee box was worth the walk and gave us a little exercise to keep our blood flowing.

When we got back to our car waiting for us on the side of the TCH, Mylan took the wheel. Forty five minutes later we were passing Gander. We recounted our conversation with Roy, the knowledgeable bartender at Erin's. We had our answers about the dual role played by the Gander International Airport thanks to Roy.

In Grand Falls-Windsor we stopped for a meal once again. Having stopped there both coming and going, we realized why these twin towns had so many restaurants; it was the natural midway point between St. John's and Corner Brook. This time we elected to play it safe and went to a Tim Horton's. With our stomachs full and the time approaching 1:30pm we again switched drivers putting me back behind the wheel. We were about half way to Corner Brook.

Chapter 24 – He Looks Harmless Enough...

About twenty minutes after stopping for lunch in Grand Falls-Windsor, on a particularly lonely and straight stretch of the TCH, Mylan and I could see a man walking on the side of the highway nearly a mile ahead. He was headed west, the same direction as we were. As we got closer we could see that he was wearing jeans and a t-shirt, remarkably little protection given the high 30s/low 40s weather.

I turned to Mylan, "What do you think? Should we see if he needs a ride?"

"Why not? He looks harmless enough."

"Okay, if he gets in, you keep an eye on him while I am driving and I will move the rear view to be able to keep an eye on him myself." I slowed the car and pulled alongside the young man with crew cut blonde hair.

Mylan stuck his head out the window, "Hey, where you headed?"

The young man replied, "Up the road a ways" with a slow, slurred delivery immediately giving evidence of his inebriation.

"Do you want a ride? We can drop you off up the road if you like," Mylan asked him politely.

I knew Mylan was gaining comfort from knowing the young man was too drunk to be any threat to us. The fact that he wore only a tee shirt contributed to my thinking that he must not have had too far to go.

"Yeah, sure. Thanks." The lightly dressed man in his early twenties moved towards the passenger side rear door of the car.

Our hitchhiker plopped into the back seat and immediately tilted his head back. The heavy smell of hard alcohol emanated from him. It was apparent that his consumption had been recent. Exactly where he had been we would never know. Mylan turned himself in his seat to engage our passenger.

"So where are you headed?"

"Home."

"How far up the road do you need to go?"

"You guys can just drop me off at the next road to the left." He answered cryptically.

I chimed in, "We would gladly drop you at your home."

"No, that's okay. I live pretty far back off the highway. One of my friends will take me home."

"Okay, as you wish." I replied more than a little befuddled.

Mylan took over guiding the conversation. "It's pretty cold out there. Weren't you cold just wearing a t-shirt?"

"No, I am used to it."

"Were you going to walk all the way home?"

"Maybe. Or somebody would give me a ride like you guys. I have a lot of friends around here."

"Doesn't seem like too many people live right around here to us."

"There is. Most of us know each other."

"What's your name?"

"Jimmy."

"Nice to meet you Jimmy. I'm Mylan. That's Timm."

"Where are you guys going?" Jimmy asked seeming to gain some measure of composure.

"Today we are headed to Corner Brook, maybe further. After that we are headed home ourselves – back to Virginia in the U.S.," Mylan shared, curious to see where that information would take the conversation.

"I've never been to the U.S." Jimmy replied curtly.

Mylan paused and looked over at me to see if I wanted to respond. I didn't. I raised my eyebrows and kind of shook my head to indicate that as far as I was concerned the conversation was all his to conduct. "Well if you get a chance there are many places to see." Mylan replied seeing if Jimmy would want to get into sightseeing opportunities in the U.S. of A. at all.

"My road is just over the next hill." Jimmy offered giving evidence that he was paying more attention to where he was than to the conversation.

"You sure we can't take you home, Jimmy?" Mylan pressed him.

"No, I have a friend just down the hill. I am going to go over there."

In a couple minutes we had indeed come to a paved road that went off to the left. That it went to the left toward the south was notable along this stretch from Grand Falls-Windsor to Corner Brook as most all the other roads off of the TCH were to the right heading north. There were no residences to be seen in any direction, but Jimmy did not seem the least bit concerned.

"Thanks for the ride," he said slowly as he got out of the car at the lonely intersection.

Mylan and I were at a loss for words. We wouldn't see him again. We would never know where he had come from or where he would go after we dropped him off. The whole experience left us both a little unsettled.

"Wow, that guy had enough alcohol in him to keep him warm or at least enough to not let him worry about it. I feel bad just dropping him off at that intersection," I grumbled, as we pulled away. "There was nothing there."

"Hey, that's what he wanted. Felt to me that he has been in that situation before. My guess is that his friend isn't too far down the hill. Just because we couldn't see a house doesn't mean there isn't one down there." Mylan rationalized trying to make me feel a little better.

"You're probably right. But do you realize that we probably drove him twelve or thirteen miles? It is just hard for me to believe that he contemplated walking that full distance from wherever he came from."

"Well he wasn't that talkative, that's for sure, so he will forever be a mystery. Maybe he works nights, maybe he doesn't work at all. Who knows? Pretty strange to be that hammered in the middle of the afternoon on a weekday. Pretty strange to be walking a half-marathon distance along the TCH. He is the only person we have seen walking since we have been in Newfoundland. But then again, maybe it isn't strange at all." Like me, Mylan was having a tough time letting this short encounter go. "One thing for sure – I am going to remember that guy."

"Me too." I echoed.

We were just a little more than a couple hours outside of Corner Brook.

Chapter 25 – Corner Brook

After dropping off our enigmatic hitchhiker, Mylan and I discussed our options for getting back to Virginia once we dropped our rental car off in Portland. We also discussed our options for the remainder of the day once we had met the ship in Corner Brook. We decided that after seeing the men on Ivan Gorthon for the last time we would have dinner somewhere in Corner Brook and then head down to Channel-Port-aux-Basques to get on the next ferry, whenever that was.

Just before 5pm I took the Lewin Parkway turn off of the TCH into Corner Brook. The road into Corner Brook was a better road than the TCH itself. The four-lane parkway turned gracefully off the ridgeline and downward toward the water in a majestic right turn that gradually exposed the town and the Port of Corner Brook. The town and the harbor lay at the end of the narrow inlet of the Humber Arm off of The Bay of Islands. It was reminiscent of the view of St. John's from Signal Hill. The entry to Corner Brook was another beautiful spot on our planet Earth courtesy of Mother Nature and the industrious people of Newfoundland.

As we came around the turn Mylan and I saw the Ivan Gorthon docked at the port. To our left was downtown Corner Brook. We would explore that in some measure after visiting with the Ivan Gorthon crew. I leaned the wheel over to the right slightly to take the exit down to Riverside Drive and within a couple minutes we were parked at the dock a short walk from the Ivan Gorthon.

"They made it. We made it. Not together, but we're here together now." I shouted out after getting out of the car.

Mylan stretched after climbing out of the passenger seat and took a long look at the Ivan Gorthon. "Seems like a long time ago that we got on the ship, and almost as long since we got off it. I do want to hear about the weather they experienced getting up here."

"Well, are you ready to see who's on board and get some pictures?" I asked.

The outside temperature was hovering around freezing. "Let's put our jackets on and I need to grab my camera," Mylan said, "Then I am."

"Right as usual. It is pretty cold out here."

We pulled our winter coats from the trunk, and quickly put them on. We grabbed our cameras from the areas under our feet in the front seat where we had been keeping them most all of the time we had been in the car. This was it – the last time we would see the Ivan Gorthon, its officers and its crew.

Chapter 26 – Mission Accomplished

Mylan and I climbed the stairs to the gangway over to the deck. The gangway came across just in front of the superstructure, allowing a good look at the big front deck of the ship. The deck carried a thick layer of ice, most likely evidence of the ship's journey around Nova Scotia through the storm system we had experienced coming into Antigonish, Nova Scotia and up southwestern Newfoundland. The North Sea was known for its rough waters, and those rough seas could create enough splashes to coat the deck by themselves. Given the experience we had driving through the snow storms we strongly suspected that water and snow from the sky above was likely the cause of the thick layer of ice. No one greeted us as we came onto the ship, so we decided to visit our stateroom to have one last look at it. We took a quick look in to firm up our memories. Then we climbed the stairs up to the chartroom and bridge deck of the superstructure. There, finally, we discovered a member of the crew – good ol' George Prudehomme. George was dressed in sweatpants, a t-shirt and flip-flops. If we had not just come in from the cold, we might have thought the Ivan Gorthon was docked in Florida, looking at George.

I caught George's attention with a shout. "Hey George. We just got on board. Where is everybody?"

George turned around and let out a big smile. "Hey Timm, hey Mylan. How the heck are you guys?"

Mylan jumped in. "We are doing great, George. We had quite the adventure getting here and we had a full day of action in St. John's yesterday. It feels weird to be back on the ship actually. How was the weather for you getting here?"

"It was pretty rough coming around Nova Scotia late Sunday, Monday and early Tuesday. Did you see the front deck? We picked up a pretty good load of ice out there getting through the snow and the high seas. You should feel fortunate you got off in Portland and missed all that." George laughed sarcastically.

"Well, George, we didn't exactly avoid the weather ourselves," I replied with some sparkle in my eye. "We got slammed at the end of the day we headed out of Portland. Saturday - right Mylan? It was actually early Sunday just after midnight. We had gotten up to Nova Scotia and were attempting to get all the way to North Sydney when we hit a near white out snow storm just before Antigonish. We ended up stopping in Antigonish for the night. We missed the afternoon ferry on Sunday and ended up taking the overnight ferry to Channel-Port-aux-Basques to get in on Monday morning, and then, Bam! We were in another white out snow storm right off the ferry!"

"We followed a snow plow for nearly four hours out of Channel-Port-aux-Basques before we broke into the clear," Mylan added, "After that the weather was pretty nice, over 50 in St. John's on Tuesday. You might have had to take your shirt off there, George!"

George and I both laughed at Mylan's surprise poke at George's light clothing in the freezing air of Corner Brook.

George pulled us back to the present by answering the original question. "I think most of the crew is below decks rigging for offload. I would think they are about done and will break for dinner before too long."

"What about the officers?" I asked curious if any of them were around.

"Larsson is directing the rigging. I think Captain Svensson is in his office or his stateroom. I just saw him not too long ago. Svard and Johansson went ashore I am pretty sure. If I am right I don't think they are coming back until just before we get underway again," George answered covering all four of the ship's officers in short order.

"Well, George, can we get some pictures of you?" Mylan asked realizing that we would only have a limited amount of time to talk to the rest of the crew before they took dinner.

"Of course," George replied.

We took turns taking pictures of George, and pictures with George, before heading down to the captain's office to see if we could catch Captain Svensson. A quick knock on the door of Captain Svensson's office and we were in luck.

"Captain! We told you we would see you in Corner Brook and here we are!" I blurted out as Mylan and I came in the door.

"Gentlemen! So good to see you made it." Captain Svensson exclaimed as he rose from his chair behind his desk. "How has your trip been since leaving Portland? What have you been doing? Please come sit down and tell me about your last few days. We have some time before dinner."

"If you didn't hear from your port agent in Portland, we had to spend a little time with Customs before we got over to the airport to rent our car," Mylan began. "Once we got our rental car we came back to get the lobsters. How did that turn out Captain? Did Miko cook them up for everybody?"

"Oh he did. Everybody really enjoyed the lobster. Miko made a soup with a couple of them and boiled the others. Everybody that wanted some got some. That was a very nice gesture on your part." Captain Svensson replied. "Please do continue with your story."

Mylan continued telling the captain of our travails and experiences similarly to how we had shared with George. Svensson was most interested in our time in St. John's so we added the most detail on the full day there. With the day in and around St. John's recounted Mylan paused for a second. "And after a good night's rest last night we took off for Corner Brook mid-morning today and now here we are."

"It seems you guys had quite the adventure getting up here by car and had a good time in St. John's as well." the captain reflected, "It is good to see you back on the ship. You must feel good to have made it up here. So are you headed back to Virginia now?"

"We are thinking that after we say our goodbyes to the rest of the crew we will grab some dinner in town and then head down to Port-aux-Basques." I answered. "We may have to spend the night before the next ferry leaves. We will see."

"Obviously we have the drive from North Sydney back to Portland," Mylan interjected. "We will drop the rental car off at the airport in Portland and then figure out the cheapest way to get back to Virginia from there. I doubt we will fly back. Tickets are way too expensive when you book same day. We will probably take a train or a bus. We will figure that out when we get there."

"Well, I hope you are happy you rode the Ivan Gorthon for as long as you did," the captain replied in a gentlemanly way that was beyond his years. "I know the crew has been wondering about you. I think they will be coming out of the cargo hold in a couple minutes. Why don't you get down to the main deck and wait for the guys? I am sure they will be very happy to see you both one last time."

"Well, Captain, thank you again for letting us have this wonderful experience," I said as Mylan and I stood. "Neither of us will ever forget our four days on the ship and the adventure we had on it and after we got off."

"I am grateful as well," Mylan added. "And from what George told us about the weather the ship went through, I have to believe that it was a good thing that we took your advice to disembark in Portland. Good luck with your career, Captain."

With a couple of firm handshakes we left the captain's office and climbed down the ladder to the main deck. Just as we got down to the main deck, Piotr, Surgei and Boris appeared from the other side of the superstructure. There were brief expressions of surprise as the men saw us standing right in front of them just as they came out onto the main deck. We quickly moved towards one another to shake hands.

After recounting the story of our last few days to Piotr, Surgei and Boris, and hearing their telling of the trip the Ivan Gorthon had taken to get to Corner Brook, we all took turns posing for pictures and taking pictures. With several photos on each of our cameras, Mylan and I shook the hands of all the crewmembers there on deck and turned to leave the Ivan Gorthon for the final time.

As we walked away from the ship, Mylan turned to me. "What a great bunch of guys. What a different lifestyle from what we have had and will have in our lives."

I contemplated Mylan's thought. "You are so right, MD. I enjoyed it immensely but it is not a lifestyle for me. As much as I love the ocean, I like terra firma much more for all the things that come with it, like being around family, eating at restaurants, watching sports on TV, gardening, etcetera."

"Let's go get dinner, brother," Mylan suggested firmly. "I think we deserve to really treat ourselves tonight."

Chapter 27 – The Journey Home

After a wonderful steak and seafood dinner in Corner Brook, Mylan and I made the drive down to Channel-Port-aux-Basques. Compared to the trip up behind the snowplow a few days earlier the drive south on a clear TCH seemed relatively short. When we got there, we first stopped at the ferry terminal to find out when the next ferry to North Sydney was leaving. The morning ferry departed at 7:30 am with the lineup forming at 6:30 am. It was nearly 10 pm so we found a nearby hotel to get some sleep. The room had two queen beds separated by only a few feet. It would be a race to fall asleep. We were both exhausted from the long day on the road interrupted only by our brief stop at Terra Nova and the three hour stop in Corner Brook. Mylan won the duel to fall asleep. I therefore had the pleasure of falling to sleep with Mylan's rhythmic snoring in the background.

At 6am Mylan's travel alarm went off. Motivated to make the ferry and buoyed by a full night's rest we got out of bed quickly and got going. We were in line at 6:45 am and loaded by 7:30 am. This time the ferry was running a little late. The Thursday morning ferry ride across the channel took about six hours. I had time at virtually every viewing station on the ferry between visits to the ferry's restaurant for some uninspiring food. Mylan spent some time viewing the ocean with me but spent the majority of the trip reading. By virtue of our loading position we were off the ferry near the beginning and we were on the road in North Sydney by 1:45 pm.

We drove the same route back out of North Sydney that we had taken to get up there. Just by crazy coincidence daylight ran out near Truro for a second time. We drove all of New Brunswick and Maine in the dark. Crossing the border back into the United States was only slightly more rigorous than crossing into Canada had been. We turned the car in after midnight at the airport and found a hotel near the airport to crash. We woke up without an alarm the next morning sometime after 8am.

Upon awaking in Portland we inquired at the front desk of the hotel about catching the train and were told that Amtrak had shut down the line north of Boston due to heavy ice on the tracks and continuing ice storms.   Winter weather was rearing its ugly head once again. Undeterred, Mylan had the front desk call over to Greyhound to see if buses were still running south. The message from Greyhound was yes, come on down to the station, we will get you to Boston.

So a short cab ride to the Greyhound station and a short wait for the next southbound bus and we were again on the road. This time neither of us had to drive. We sat near the front of the bus to observe the road and the weather. Not more than twenty minutes out of Portland it started to rain, or snow; it was both really. The mixed conditions turned out to be hell on the windshield wipers and the bus driver was forced to stop about every five to ten minutes to knock the accumulated ice off of the wiper blades. Stopping every five to ten minutes combined with top speeds of just over 20 mph on the slushy/icy I-95 made for a lengthy trip to Boston. We had gotten on the bus around 1pm in Portland. We finally arrived in Boston around 6pm. It had taken approximately five hours to cover what would have, in good conditions, normally taken two hours.

In Boston we got off the bus and got our bags from the storage area under the seating area of the bus. Our plan was to transfer to Amtrak and proceed south to Richmond by train. We walked across the South Station lobby to the Amtrak ticket counter. There was no line at the ticket counter which should have raised a red flag. The agent at the counter told us that Amtrak had just shut down the line from Boston to New York due to worsening weather along the route. We just couldn't catch a break.

Back to Greyhound we trudged feeling even more snake bitten by the weather than we had on Monday getting off the ferry in Channel-Port-aux-Basques. Fortunately, the wait for the next bus to Penn Station in New York was not long. By 7pm we were back on the bus heading south on I-95 again. Unfortunately the weather followed us. The ride to New York was much like the ride to Boston with repeated stops to knock the ice off the windshield wipers and speeds well below what would be normal in good conditions. What would have normally taken a little under four hours took over six hours, and we arrived in New York just after 1am. We had been on Greyhound for twelve hours. Thankfully by the time we got to New York the sleet/snow/rain mix had turned to rain. South of New York Amtrak was up and running and there were seats available on the Northeast Regional departing at 3am.

I called Libbie from Washington DC at 7am during the short stop there to let her know that we would be arriving at the Staples Mill Amtrak station in Richmond at 10am. It was January 9th, Saturday. School started up again on Monday. Our final semester at Darden lay ahead. Mylan and I would get a couple days of watching the NFL football playoffs, this time at home, to rest up from our adventure to Newfoundland.

Epilogue – Reflections on the Adventure

Whenever I look back at our adventure on the Ivan Gorthon and off it in our rental car, I am always struck by how events unfurled, how one thing led to another. There was the unlikely dare that a proud logistics manager answered, and two adventurous friends actually taking him up on the offer of a wintertime ride to Newfoundland on a merchant freighter, and then there were the overindulgences of a New Year's Eve of drinking, which had a grueling impact on the trip. Those were the big things. The original plan of riding the ship to Corner Brook and maybe having a couple days to see Newfoundland was altered so dramatically that my friend Mylan and I had to rent a car in Portland, Maine to get to Newfoundland. Our revised goal was to meet the ship in Corner Brook on our way back from St. John's.

Then the snow storms delayed our progress and increased our stress levels significantly. Each delay resulted in an impact on what lay ahead in our spontaneous schedule, each event compounding the other. The series of events were as real a testament to the Butterfly Effect as any I have ever experienced in my life over any relatively short amount of time. The period of time for our Three Legs to Newfoundland adventure was inside of a week. The entire trip was a little longer than a week and the tail end of the trip, specifically our journey back from Portland to Richmond, with weather again impacting the method and pace of our movement, was enough to make us never want to travel up north during the winter again.

As for specific memories of the Ivan Gorthon and its crew I always come back to the incredibly young captain and his concerns for Mylan's health and safety. I think that he really would have preferred that we had never come aboard. I am left to wonder who at the shipping company made the decision to let us ride the ship. Who was my wife's workmate, the shipping and logistics manager, talking to who ultimately turned my dare into our reality?

Captain Svensson was a good man who was fairly new to his job and his responsibilities. I wonder how much he remembers today, fourteen years later, of our brief ride on his ship back in 1998/9. The crew, mostly Polish sailors, certainly knew how to have a good time, certainly knew how to consume ridiculous quantities of vodka, and certainly took their jobs seriously and worked hard.

We got the required safety training, were shown around all the parts of the ship we cared to see, and were made to feel as much at home on the ship as could possibly be expected. But since we were not given any job to do, Mylan and I quickly felt superfluous, which is exactly what we were, and that is what ultimately made the decision to disembark from the ship, as Captain Svensson strongly recommended, a far easier one to make than had we been given practical work to do.

Traveling in the northeast of the U.S.A. and in the Canadian Maritimes in January carries with it obvious risks related to weather. Most anybody would spot you that stipulation going in. That being a given, I still think we got far more than our fair share of bad weather on that stretch from Saturday late night on January 2nd outside Antigonish, Nova Scotia and Monday morning, January 4th from Channel-Port-aux-Basques to outside Corner Brook in Newfoundland to our miserable day of bus travel from Portland, Maine to New York City on Friday January 8th. Yes, after the snow in western Newfoundland we escaped the snow heading east and we had pretty decent weather the remainder of our time on the island. In St. John's, despite overcast skies much of the time, the temperatures were at freezing or above – all things considered pretty good for early January.

When we saw the ice on the deck of the Ivan Gorthon in the port of Corner Brook we knew the ship and the crew had come through the storms we had driven through. It was what Piotr and the captain had expected, given the information they had been given that Saturday evening in Portland. It was why Captain Svensson thought it prudent to suggest we disembark in Portland. I am glad we did get off the ship. The journey to Newfoundland was more memorable thanks to our renting the car in Portland and driving up. Had we not done that, we would not have run into the snow storm outside Antigonish. We wouldn't have missed the afternoon ferry and watched NFL playoff football on Sunday in North Sydney, and we wouldn't have gotten into Channel-Port-aux-Basques right into the teeth of yet another near white out snow storm. It truly was a series of crazy outcomes like falling dominos, each impacting the next. That we were in such a spontaneous mode all throughout the trip from Portland on also led to amazing discoveries in unexpected places: the restaurant in Torbay with its roots in Richmond, Virginia; musicians practicing their craft at Erin's Pub; a drunken hitchhiker in the middle of the nowhere.

Finally, I remember all the things that were, and likely still are, so Canadian, so Nova Scotian and so Newfie in our experience. Number one amongst all these was the line from the gate agent at the North Sydney ferry terminal, "That was just a guess." That was so non-American for two American tourists accustomed to depend on a reliable schedule for our cut-it-close, squeeze as much in as possible in the least amount of time possible, approach.

Then there were the friendly people, at every turn – Richard, the owner of The Roses; Teresa, the breakfast cook at The Roses; Roy, the bartender at Erin's; the waitresses at the restaurant in North Sydney and in Corner Brook; the border crossing agent in St. Stephen. There simply were no exceptions all along the way.

My greatest memory of the adventure is being with my great friend, a man I think of as a brother today. Since the trip up to Newfoundland our friendship continued and we remain very close. We were forever linked by the experience. I feel blessed to have been able to have experienced all that we shared on the trip, what we now refer to as our Great Newfoundland Adventure. The time Mylan and I shared on the Ivan Gorthon was a once in a lifetime experience. The beauty of St.

John's and Newfoundland and the wonderful, incredibly friendly people of Newfoundland and the other Maritime provinces are what made the trip one for a lifetime.

Author biography

Timm Bechter was born in New Haven, Connecticut in 1963, the first of four children. His parents moved the growing family back and forth between Connecticut and Vermont as Timm's father taught economics and mathematics at Middlebury College and Connecticut College for Women and worked on his PhD dissertation at Yale over seven years. In 1970 the family moved to Liberty, Missouri, a suburb of Kansas City. An athlete growing up, Timm's prowess on the baseball field helped him get into the U.S. Naval Academy in 1981 after graduating from Liberty High School. Timm served in the U.S. Navy upon graduation in 1985 and was a division officer on board the USS Vandegrift (FFG-48) out of Long Beach, California from 1987-1990. He married his wife Elizabeth "Libbie" in 1990 after being honorably discharged from the navy. He worked as an environmental professional and plant manager for a lightweight aggregate producer in Virginia before attending The University of Virginia's Darden Graduate School of Business from 1997-1999. Upon graduating from Darden he began a 12-year career as an equity analyst before leaving the profession in 2011 to become an author and private investor. Timm and Libbie make their home in Goochland County Virginia.

Made in the USA
Middletown, DE
29 May 2019